*B*EYOND **40** A CRES

&

A NOTHER

P AIR OF S HOES

For
Smart Sisters
Who Think Too Much
and
Do Too Little
About Their Money

P AMELA A YO Y ETUNDE

M ARA B ELL A B OOKS

Marabella Books

We would like to hear from you. If you have comments or suggestions or you would like to order additional copies of this book, please write or call us at:

Marabella Books
4096 Piedmont Avenue PMB 307
Oakland, California 94611
510.337.3262
http://www.smartsisters.com

Book design by Tracey Scott
Cover art and design by Randolph Belle,
www.oaklandart.com

ISBN 1-928775-00-4

10 9 8 7 6 5 4 3 2

Dedicated to sisters who revel in the journey

to self-discovery and awareness

Table of Contents

I. THE ROAD WE HAVE TRAVELED

II. BREAKING THE CHAINS: WEALTH DISORIENTATION SYNDROME

III. ON THE PATH TO WEALTH

Acknowledgments

My deepest gratitude goes to a number of people for a variety of time commitments, feedback, insights and emotional support.

To Carla Moss who told me that she had read many books on financial matters, none of them addressing the concerns I raised. To members of BW2000 for sharing their information needs.

To all those who read early, early drafts and gave me "straight no chaser" critiques: Jackie Brown, Gail Spann, Kavita Ramdas, Tracey Williams, Ramona Hadley, Maria DeMarco and Victor's Café Reading Circle.

To Maryann Hrichak who showed me how this book was relevant to women of many ethnicities. To Deloris Scott, for telling me how she really felt after she recovered from the experience.

To Felicia Poe who was generous with her time, research skills, and encouragement. To Banshee Girl Productions for their marketing advice. To Susan Harrow for entrée into her network. To Kimberlee Bogen for her all-around support and legal expertise.

To Tracey Scott for her commitment to the Marabella Books partnership.

And to Paul Travis for being my first client.

Introduction

You have taken the first step towards awareness and creating a personal econo-culture by opening this book. If you are accountable to yourself, you will read it and evaluate whether it applies to you. If you feel some responsibility toward others, you will send a copy to a sister to help her on the path to recasting herself. I encourage you to contact any organization concerned about the lives of African-American women and encourage them to add economic empowerment to their agenda.

We know how to organize for change. There will not be a national dialogue on the economic freedom of the African American woman until we desire financial freedom and move with each other in that direction. Even during the Great Depression in 1930, when prospects were dim for much of America, fifty African American women exerted their economic power by forming the Detroit Housewives League. Within four years membership had grown to 10,000 and they had affected the lives of countless more. When sisters have gathered together to make changes, we have succeeded.

As I break the rules, please don't sentence me to "sell-out's jail" or condemn me to "Oreo purgatory" unless at the end of the book, I have said nothing of value to any sister.

The ways in which we have discussed money has not led us to having more. So, try something different because there is a chance that you may find yourself, one fine day, living the rest of your life without financial worry.

I want you to be in the best financial position possible to help yourself, your family, and friends, so they can do the same for themselves and their loved ones. I often tell my clients, as I am telling you, that I do not settle for you doing less than you can. When a worthy politician asks for your help, I want you to be able to support her or him. When your favorite charity needs your help, I want you to be charitable. I want you to be in the best financial position to help someone, starting with yourself.

40 acres and another pair of shoes.
It is the mentality and behavior of hoping and buying.
40 acres and another pair of shoes.
Hope and buy. Hope and buy. Hope and buy.

If more money is what you desire, begin by keeping this book wherever you keep your bills. Refer to it every time you pay your creditors. Let it serve as a reminder to pay yourself every time you pay everyone else.

If you want other African-American women to have money, I invite you to buy copies for them. Why buy rather than share? One, you keep your book as your reminder. Two, they keep their books as reminders. Three, *I will donate a portion of the proceeds from the sale of this book to organi-*

zations dedicated to improving the financial lives of all African-Americans through financial education.

In a way, this book is one I wish someone had written for me while I was in college. Like yourself, perhaps, I have waited on others to remedy our financial ills, and in the absence of corrective action, we have drowned our pain with things. *Beyond 40 Acres and Another Pair of Shoes* is an attitude check. You will know that reading *Beyond 40 Acres and Another Pair of Shoes* has been beneficial if you begin to see and hear wealth opportunities differently, and take advantage of them.

We have a Code of Silence about money that benefits no one. Let's change that for each other's sake. Don't keep a good thing a secret! I feel confident that upon using this book as it is intended, we will begin a national discourse on money, and will begin to have more money as a result of our efforts. I wish you all the best in your quest for financial success!

I. *The Road We Have Traveled*

134 years ago

Freed slaves, with no money,

were promised 40 acres and a mule

to create their own wealth.

30 years ago

Dr. Martin Luther King Jr. organized

the Poor People's March to bring attention

to the "economic injustices"

inflicting "deep social

and economic wounds"

in the lives of African-Americans

and poor people.

30 years later...

1. *The Code of Silence*

Poverty continues to be one of the major problems in the African-American community. The National Urban League, the NAACP, the Black Radical Congress, the Presidential Panel on Race and leaders agree that a disproportionate number of us are bleeding for the want of financial security in a capitalist society. Conversely, many of us have been taught that it is inappropriate to talk about our personal financial situation with others. We have been taught that it is even more inappropriate to ask others about their personal finances.

Through the centuries, we have created and maintained a Code of Silence that makes it difficult, at best, and impossible, at worst, to talk with each other about money. With a shared history as slaves, sharecroppers, low-paid domestic workers, low-paid clerks, low-paid hotel workers, under-paid government workers, low-paid factory workers, and low-paid teachers, the Code of Silence served to protect us from having to talk about how little money we made. The Code was easy to maintain because, by and large, there was no money to talk about. Today, more of us have more money, therefore it's time to break the Code of Silence.

I have advised many people about what to do with their money. My experience as an African-American woman and a financial advisor to sisters has told me that we have great difficulty talking about money. As a consequence, we have an even greater difficulty building wealth. As a life-long advocate for human rights, I believe that economic rights are human rights. In advocating for human rights, oftentimes rules and laws are broken. In order to create the wealth we desire, we must break the "law of cultural norms" and discuss openly what we do with our money.

This book is a financial security ambulance (running through red lights and stop signs in an emergency) Dr. King spoke of in his speech on economic security. There was an emergency then, and there is an emergency, now. Thirty years from now, the emergency will have reached catastrophic proportions, unless we reverse the trend of the poor becoming poorer. We can do so if we agree that we will not punish each other for running the red lights and stop signs. In other words, break the rules of ordinary conduct, discourse, and beliefs around our money by breaking the Code of Silence.

In running the red lights, I am purposefully going to break rules to share some thoughts with you, the sister who may be thinking too much and doing too little about her money. Here are some of the unwritten rules (depending on your viewpoint), I will probably break from time to time:

Money Code of Silence

1. Don't discuss dirty laundry in public;
2. Don't critique sisters in public;
3. Don't critique our heros and sheros in public;
4. Don't critique the church in private or public;
5. Blame the White Man for our economic woes;
6. Don't tell anyone what you do with your money;
7. Don't trust financial institutions;
8. Don't advocate capitalism for African-Americans;
9. Don't suggest African-Americans consider fiscal conservatism because it sounds like Republicanism.
10. We have been subjugated as a people for too long, therefore don't give our oppressors any more ammunition to cause additional pain.

In light of all these rules (and I am sure there are more), there is no wonder why we have a Code of Silence around our money matters. Each rule is connected to an issue around how we deal with money. I realize the risk in critiquing our money habits. I risk being labeled a heretic, a capitalist, a Black capitalist, a sell-out, an Oreo, a lackey – you name it. The risk of being called something I am not does not outweigh the financial benefits to you and our community. As you will discover, wealth building, at its most fundamental core, is about taking risks. Whether you know it or not, you have been labeled risk averse by the fact that you are African-American and female. The Code of Silence has not allowed us to fully question or challenge whether this belief is factual (studies have shown that we behave conservatively). The combination of beliefs, cultural norms, habits, the Code of Silence and the present-day economic situation, requires that we examine ourselves and our money with a heightened sense of urgency and with no regard for politically-correct speech, tip-toeing or whitewashing. We must pull off the kid gloves, pull up our sleeves and maybe even don boxing gloves to change our culture around money.

Many of my clients define financial success by the ability to buy things. As a community, we generate $400 billion of disposable income, but our buying power is diminishing. The U.S. Census Department has reported that between 1992 and 1995, one-third of the nation lived below the poverty line at some point during those three years. United for A Fair Economy, a not-for-profit educational organization, notes that three out of four U.S. workers have lost economic ground.

Traditional indicators like low inflation and low unemployment are no longer adequate barometers for measuring the extent of economic inequities. The longest running bull (stock buying) market came to an end with the fall of Asian, Russian, and Brazilian markets abroad, and pessimism at home around President Clinton's ability to lead. What does all this have to do with you, when all you're trying to do is enjoy life? Both the economy and the Code of Silence challenge the quality of your economic life. If the wealthy are becoming nervous, wouldn't that indicate that you might have reason to at least pause and think about your money? Yes, that is exactly what you are doing right now.

As you take time to pause and think about money, think about this – I want you to have more money. Let me say it again, "I want you to have more money, not because I am financially dependent on you, but because I know you can better fulfill your dreams with more money." When is the last time anyone said that to you? Sisters don't often include personal economics in our repertoire of nurturing because the Code of Silence says, "It's none of your business." Wealth is a human right worthy of achieving and protecting, therefore I am asking you to make personal finance your business.

As my clients know, I rejoice in them getting ahead financially. When I see the net worth of my clients increase, it makes me happy because I know they are achieving their goals and closer to realizing their dreams. I am saddened, as any caring sister would be, when I see my sister-clients refusing to take control over their financial destinies. Why am I saddened? It's not my money, right? Absolutely. It's not about the money, it's about the inability to fulfill dreams. I decided to write this book upon observing highly unusual behavior exhibited to me by intelligent African-American women faced with the opportunity to make money on their money, thereby fulfilling their dreams. Generally speaking, I have seen confident, articulate, smart women turn to mush when contemplating their money matters. Many, but not all of us, become indecisive, weak, inarticulate, slow, non-committal, confused, angry, and irrational around money decisions. This is evidence of what I call **Wealth Disorientation Syndrome (WDS)**.

In contemplating what I wanted to call this phenomenon, I struggled with the criticism I am sure to receive. "We don't need anyone judging us, especially a sister." This is not a judgment, this is a metaphor. How do we break the Code of Silence, when we have not created the vocabulary for doing so? We cannot. This book will provide the vocabulary to break the Code of Silence.

I wrote this book specifically for smart African-American women. Why not *Beyond 40 Acres and Another Pair of Shoes: For* Dumb *Sisters*? Right! Books written for "dummies" seem to sell well perhaps because readers assume that the information is so simple any idiot could become wealthy overnight. I prefer to appeal to the intelligence in you. Smart sisters know that in order to become smarter, you have to invest time and sometimes money in the acquisition of information. With the right information, smart sisters can apply it to their situations. Knowledge will be gained and hopefully passed on to the sisters who don't think much, but are just smart enough to know when to take advice from someone like yourself – a financially-successful sister. I hope I inspire you to turn to your sisters, smart or otherwise, and say, "I want you to have more money."

Imagine if each of us called each sister-friend to say, "I want you to have more money." You would also receive calls from your sister-friends saying, "I want you to have more money." Initially, we might be met with some resistance and resentment. "What do you mean you want me to have more money? Are you suggesting I don't have enough?" Most of what we know about money is negative. If you doubt what I am saying, name the one classic soul hit about money that probably most sisters in their 30s and 40s know. I'll give you a hint. It was written by Gamble, Huff, and Jackson. Do you need another hint? It was sung by the O'Jays. The song is entitled *For the Love of Money*. If you know the song, you probably recall the hypnotic beat, the reverberating crescendo of "Money, Money, Money, Money." The O'Jays sang about the evils of money. They called money "mean green" that leads some people to steal from their mothers, rob their brothers, lie and cheat, engage in prostitution, and cause mental insanity. They end the song with the warning, "People, don't let money fool you."

For the Love of Money was one of my favorite songs! Was it yours? How did it affect your attitude toward money? Much of what we feel about money has to do with the outward artistic expressions of the value of money in our lives. For example, in a more recent concert at the Apollo, the now deceased Notorious B.I.G. and Sean "Puff Daddy" Combs, threw cash money into the audience during their rap performance. Cash, gold, and diamonds play a big part in the imagery of rap music. Twenty years ago, money was evil. Today, it is "EAZY": easy come, easy go. It is time to examine the variety of factors that influence the way we feel about money.

It's probably not fair to say that we never talk about our personal finances. Unfortunately when we break the Code of Silence, we usually talk about our poor cash flow, high consumer debt, and exhaustion from working too much and having too little to show for it. Though these are realities for some of us, many of us say we have no money knowing good and well we do. We are just used to saying, "Girl, I don't have any money." If we had more positive experiences with money – having it when we need it, the ability to pay bills on time, the willingness to open mail from financial institutions, reading and understanding statements, watching our investments fluctuate and grow over time, getting insurance proceeds when a loved one dies, and getting benefits when we become disabled – a call from a sister saying, "I want you to have more money" would be welcomed with enthusiasm. The Code of Silence, created over time, supported by acquiescence to cultural norms, validated by artistic expression, coupled with negative financial experiences, and fortified by the lack of advertisements by financial institutions in the publications we read most, can lead one to experience a cumulative depletion of one's spirit or awareness around her personal finances.

Imagine you are sitting at home, minding your own business. Suddenly, you get a call from a sister-friend who says, "Hey girl, what's up? I was looking at my portfolio and I thought I'd give you a call to find out how you're doing with your investments." How would you react? Many sisters react to me with automatic resistance because if we work together, I am eventually going to tell her what to do with her money (anything less would constitute an unmet expectation worthy of her severing our working relationship). Ironically, we are both open and closed to taking advice about our money. Sisters tell me consistently, "I would have had more money had someone told me sooner what to do with it." While I am trying to advise them, many sisters are thinking or feeling, "I don't want her telling me what to do with my money." What are we doing to ourselves when we try to convince ourselves that things would have been different years ago, then we resist making things different today for the future? Imagine yourself 10, 20, or 30 years from now saying, "I would have had more money if someone had just told me..." Starting today, I want you to have no regrets about the decisions you will make about your money.

We have lived most of our lives with the **Code of Silence** about our money. When you reach out to a sister to say, "Hey, how are you doing with your money?" remember that even though we don't speak much about money with each other, many of us have had thoughts about money. We have heard in our heads the pounding sounds of desire for financial freedom. Years of drowning thoughts of more money with no verbal outlet, but "Girl, you know I have no money" can often erupt into defensive and contentious conversations. Know that it's only a knee-jerk response to a topic we aren't used to discussing regularly.

There is a possibility that your sisters won't hear you when you say, "I want you to have more money." They may opt out of the conversation completely, postponing financial decisions until a "better" day. But better days are always too far away. *Today* is the best day to contemplate and act on financial matters. If we do not break the Code of Silence we will lose, and the only winners will be manufacturers who rely on our purchases for their profits. We have served our nation well (economically) through more than 200 years of slave labor, underpaid labor, and as consumers. It is time for us to exercise our fundamental human rights by taking on new roles as investors rather than just consumers. We cannot make decisions about how our economy affects us and others until we deal with our own personal financial development and growth.

We can be stronger, I want us to be stronger and more influential than we are. This may not happen until we acknowledge the factors that weaken our resolve around money. In this respect, some portions of *Beyond 40 Acres and Another Pair of Shoes* may be painful for you. Do not despair. Through our weaknesses, I will reveal our strengths in ways you probably didn't know we had.

I wrote this book because most information written about money is not written with you in mind. Of course, you are not physically prohibited from reading anything on the shelf. It is not to say that financial professionals who write do not care about us. I wrote this book because only a few of us in the profession know that we have been singing Bessie Smith's blues about "Nobody Knows You When You're Down and

Out" for far too long. I wrote this book because my clients have yet to read anything like this. I wrote *Beyond 40 Acres and Another Pair of Shoes,* because you deserve more money than you have, and you have the right to know about the opportunities available to you. You have the wisdom to know what you need for sustenance, shelter and protection. You also know that no food or shelter comes for free. Your sister-friends and sister advisors want you to have more money. Period.

The purpose of this book is to help you become more attracted to the financial information and professionals genuinely willing and able to assist you. If the poor are getting poorer, and the rich richer, what is happening to those of us in the middle (which includes most of us)? The choice is yours, unless you choose to leave it to someone else. In order to exercise the choice to control your financial destiny, you can avoid becoming a member of the *future poor.* All it takes is an adjustment in your attitude, some time, and a little money.

2. It's the Economy, Girlfriend!

No matter what your present financial state, the fact is most of us are living lives of **financial paradox** in the U.S. According to the United Nations, we live in the richest industrialized nation with the highest human poverty index. Our collective lives of financial paradox lead to confusion about what wealth is and how financially successful an African-American woman can become. You need not be confused, but be certain that your destiny includes financial security, and wealth – *if you want it.*

Let's begin by breaking rule number eight: capitalism should not be advocated for African-Americans. Capitalism is defined in many ways, but for many political progressives (if I may use the label) capitalism is the reason why African-Americans have less money than Whites. "**Popular capitalism**," as described by U.S. Ambassador to France Felix G. Rohatyn is:

A highly advanced market system in a democratic country with large participation by the population in the ownership of capital assets, coupled with an active and intelligent Government that provides an advanced social safety net and sophisticated regulatory systems, in a law-abiding culture.

Under this definition sisters and brothers should increase substantially our participation in the ownership of capital assets. George Orwell wrote, "poverty annihilates the future." As much poverty as there has been and continues to be in our community, it is no wonder why we are where we are, and why so many people possess so little hope that we will be better off tomorrow.

The financial paradox (living in the richest and poorest industrialized nation) plays itself out in the acquisition of "things" at the expense of acquiring money. You may be able to buy what you think wealthy people buy, but you may not be able to save and invest what the wealthy set aside and therefore accumulate. According to the U.S. Trust *Survey of Affluent Americans*, the top 1% of the wealthiest Americans save and invest 27% of their income, and spend 6% on healthcare and insurance. In other words, 33% goes toward their wealth building plan. If you committed 33% of your income to your plan, you'd save and invest $9,900 annually if you earn $30,000. If you earn $50,000, you would save $16,500. If you earn $75,000, you would save $24,750. If you are not committing one-third of your income to your financial plan, you are not really "living large", you're living dangerously on the edge of future financial ruin.

You may very well be living a poverty existence and not know it because you can buy what the millionaires seem to have. Looking past the images of sports and entertainment figures, most millionaires are not very glamorous. In *The Millionaire Next Door*, authors Stanley and Danko note that 25% of those surveyed have never spent more than $100 for a watch, $99 for a pair of shoes, or $285 for a suit. They could spend more, but choose not to. This super-frugality raises two questions:

1) Are these people millionaires because they do not spend much?
2) If becoming frugal does not appeal to you because it means you will feel deprived, where else can you find self-worth and abundance?

The answer to the first question is "yes." There is a correlation between accumulating wealth and not overspending. The answer to the second question is "from within."

Having money gets you closer to fulfilling your dreams. If you are experiencing a financial awakening or reawakening, and you have worked for several years and have $1,500 or less in savings and investments, you may be two paychecks away from qualifying for a welfare benefit. You may be saying to yourself, "I know I will never go without work." Now ask yourself this question, "Do you really want to work (especially for someone else) the rest of your life?" If you are like most people I advise, your answer is, "If I could retire today, I would." How prepared are you to retire today?

When is the last time you read an article or book entitled, "Times Are A Changin' and Black Women are Getting

Screwed"? Probably never, because no one has been bold enough to say it. Nevertheless, the messages are out there. The political and economic climate in our country has changed for the better for many, and those who have made gains (black and white) are openly asking why we sisters can't seem to get it together. Why all the drama? Some people have a lot more in banks, brokerage firms and insurance companies than you do. (United For A Fair Economy notes that 73% of African-Americans have less than three months' savings accumulated.) Why all the drama? Sisters are spending a lot, and griping even more about how broke we are: "Girl, you know I have no money, but I'm going to go on that cruise anyway." Why all the drama? We are living in a season of economic upheaval in the stock market. Like flowers that bloomed consistently for several years in the gardens of brokerage firms, wealth is withering and blossoming, withering and blossoming every single day. If you did not stop to smell the new money as it was growing, your lack of historical perspective may cause you to be fearful of investing. Therefore, to wait until the gardens are fertilized before you begin investing may be the worst mistake you can make with your money.

In 1929, after the stock market crashed, there was high unemployment and the climate was ripe for the introduction of welfare, social security, and other federal programs to help Americans find employment. Today, the conditions that ushered in welfare and social security are completely reversed. Those who stopped relying on the government, and began relying on corporate profits, do not see the need to devote their tax dollars to assisting others who don't save and invest their money. According to the U.S. Trust *Survey of Affluent Americans,* 69% said welfare payments other than aid to dependent children programs should be cut or eliminated entirely, and 62% said that Social Security benefits should be paid only to individuals who have paid money into the system. Do we need welfare and social security like we needed it in the past? There is no easy answer, but the general sentiment is clear, "You are on your own!" The financially paradoxical lives of African-American women weigh in the balance, and we have the power to tip the scales in our favor.

Perception is not necessarily reality, but we must examine how others view us:

> According to Jill Duerr Berrick in her book, *Faces of Poverty*, 39% of women receiving Aid to Families with Dependent Children are African American, yet media images suggest that *all* welfare mothers are African American.

We must also examine how we perceive ourselves:

> In the Ariel/Schwab Black investor survey, *Saving and Investing Among High Income Black and White Americans*, it was found that 55% of African-Americans say they are doing a fair or poor job saving money.

Those who sell us products view us as follows:

> African-American women make up 54% of the $398 billion African-American economy.

It simply cannot be true that most of us do not work and generate hundreds of billions of dollars. Therefore, it must be true that some of us work and some of us don't. Whether you work or not, if it is true that you have difficulty saving or investing your discretionary money, in the end, it doesn't matter whether you worked or not.

There is a chance that in 30 years those making $50,000 and more will be virtually in the same place as those who make less or nothing. The future poor might be you, someone who works and spends, but thinks too little about the money after it is earned.

3. *Poverty is* Not *Our Destiny*

Here's the good news (I like being the bearer of good news) *we are not predestined to enter the 21ˢᵗ century as we entered the 20ᵗʰ*. Poverty is *not* our destiny, it's just how we started our lives in the U.S.

The financial paradox has always been our collective reality. For those of us cognizant of our economic woes, the U.N. has not reported anything new about how African-Americans experience our nation. Only on a rare occasion will we be reminded that we are entitled to participate in the wealth of this nation.

There is a lot of financial information to be consumed these days: magazines on buying stocks and bonds, mutual funds books, the financial pages of daily newspapers, television and radio shows on the state of the economy and wealth opportunities, websites on the Internet and online services. Yet, we women of African descent, are not consuming our share of the readily available and affordable information. Some of us, who are consuming the information, refuse to act upon it. We are confronted with opportunities and professionals willing to help us make the most of our money, but we often reject these opportunities. Why?

Some sisters believe that relying on professional help of any kind is an admission of weakness. Yet, relying on experts in areas you are not knowledgeable about is an admission of strength and a positive step toward wealth. Over 50% of the wealthiest people in the country say they rely on investment managers, financial planners, attorneys and certified public accountants because they believe 1) they do not have enough knowledge to properly manage their finances, and 2) investments have become too complex for individuals to understand (US Trust survey). What do we really believe and why? Opinions are now just forthcoming.

We have been in this country more than 300 years, but just in 1997, the first nationwide study of African-Americans' attitudes regarding investing was conducted. 1997!? What took so long? Until recently, no one cared what we did with our money as long as we spent it. If we continue spending at the rates we do, we will continue serving our implied purpose: to make others wealthy. What the heck, if we won't work for free, we can just give our earnings away to others. I know there is a better way.

In most instances where sisters and money are spoken of in the same sentence, it is where the sister has none. Thanks to the image of the welfare mother portrayed in the media, African-American women are the only group of people considered to partake in America's wealth without giving anything in return. Volumes have been written about reforming the welfare system, welfare mothers, and the pathology of poverty.

Unfortunately, there is no image or national dialogue on the African-American woman as financially-independent. Why? Certainly we cannot expect others to raise the issue or create the image. Clearly, we have not made it an issue ourselves. Why? Many of us are broke, financially and spiritually. There are people who have very little money, but seem to be able to negotiate through life quite well. There are others who have a lot of money, and are very unhappy. Both types of people are broke. The former has no money, the latter has no spirit.

I met with a 50-year old sister the same week her son left for the military. She had raised him by herself. In his departure, her initial financial concern was that she might have to pay more in taxes because she had no dependents.

At our second meeting, she brought in a portion of her financial information. Her salary was about $50,000, she had $50,000 in her retirement account, no debts, and about $1,000 monthly unaccounted for in her budget. She had nothing in a savings account, and the amount of money in her checking account was just enough to cover her monthly fixed expenses, e.g. rent, car note. Her car was almost paid off. In three months' time, she would have about $1,300 per month in discretionary income.

In my excitement for her, I suggested she could

do a lot more with her money, such as increase her 401(k) contributions to retire in more comfort and grace. Before I stated an amount for her increase, she responded, "But I don't want to feel broke!"

This smart sister equated investing more money with feeling broke because she wanted to spend more money on herself after 18 years of caring for her son. She knows that 401(k) contributions reduce one's taxable income (her initial goal), and she knows she doesn't have nearly what she needs in her account to retire in comfort, but she was hit with a bout of Wealth Disorientation Syndrome, and never returned to my office to complete her financial plan.

This sister typifies what I see in many of us — an unawareness of self as we relate to money and materialism. Anthony de Mello, a Jesuit priest wrote a book entitled, *Awareness: The Perils and Opportunities of Reality.* The subtitle is profound in its suggestion that the road to becoming aware is not easy, because there are many opportunities for change along the path to an unknown place called reality. De Mello defines spirituality, not as religion, but as awareness. Awareness is the place you find yourself when you wake up.

In Penny Marshall's movie *Awakenings,* Robert DeNiro depicts a 40ish man who had lived in a coma-like state for 30 years until a research doctor used an experimental drug to awaken him. During his brief awakening, he learned about

life and how to appreciate it. Months later, the drug was useless and the patient returned to his coma-like state. Similarly,
sisters who think too much and do too little about their money
will wake up at different times in their lives, but the question
remains: what will cause you to awaken and stay awake?

Unfortunately, too many sisters live decades in a coma-
like state with regards to their money. After years of unin-
formed and uninterrupted bad habits, when the habit is fi-
nally called into question, sisters awaken to three conclusions:

1) There is still time to get off the road to poverty;
2) I can put wealth building off until I make my next
   purchase(s);
3) There is no time left and I am destined to live the rest
   of my life in poverty.

The sister who has no hope for generating her own wealth
and does not read the entire book, especially the sections entitled Wealth Disorientation Syndrome and Financial Hopscotch and the Teeter Totter effect, will look to others for
help. Her consciousness about money will disappear, and
she will return to her coma-like state, never again to experience a financial awareness or awakening. The sister who is
procrastinating on building wealth is not interested in having
more money right now. Unless she reads the sections entitled Procrastination, Procrastination and Psyche!, she will
wake up one day in her life where the hopeless woman is
today. The sister who recognizes that today is the time to act
on wealth building opportunities, but doubts her ability to

make good decisions can benefit from the section entitled Risk Measurement.

If you consider yourself a sister with no money, yet you are willing to change your attitude and behavior (if necessary) in order to have more, *and* you are willing to move money to the top of your priority list, you must reshuffle whatever thoughts you presently have about money and how you are going to get it.

I want to help you determine whether you are broke beyond repair and whether your inadequate financial preparation has anything to do with a lack of spiritual connectedness to yourself, our ancestors, our sisters and brothers and our future generation. If the money you generate is all about you and your needs, you may never find the purpose that leads to the desire for abundance in its various forms. For the sake of us all, I beg you to step out of yourself for the next two hours and ask yourself, "What does it really mean to have more?"

4. *Why 40 Acres and a Mule?*

Selective memory, repressed memories, and collective amnesia contribute to our inability to effect change in our economic lives. As an example, many African-Americans take issue with the Nation of Islam on many levels, but most of us respect their entrepreneurial drive (even if we tease them on occasion about their bean pies). We tease them because, unlike the Nation of Islam, too many of us dismiss the importance of history as a galvanizing force.

I talk about slavery in the context of financial planning, because the history of oppression can motivate us to be better off, and provides a context for discussions with sisters who argue that money means nothing to them. The legacy of slavery is that we are supposed to forget our history. In forgetting, we lose the power of the past to motivate us to change our future. As a result, slavery and the slave mentality continue to build the belief that money means nothing to us and therefore we are willing to settle for less.

Let's fast rewind 134 years ago to The Emancipation Proclamation and the time when slaves were informed that they were no longer slaves. According to Eric Foner in his book, *Reconstruction: America's Unfinished Revolution 1863-1877*, General William Tecumseh Sherman made the promise that slaves would be restored or made whole with 40 acres of land and a mule to work the land. One thousand families received their 40 acres on Skiddaway Island in Georgia. Shortly thereafter, President Abraham Lincoln overturned General Sherman's promise.

Today, the demand of 40 acres resonates well with many, but I suspect that the promise, even if it had been carried out, was never meant to put us on equal footing with White people. Whites had to replace free human labor with something. So, they turned to industry while directing us toward agriculture. Now, even the African-American farmers suffer with discrimination 134 years later, claiming that the U. S. Department of Agriculture discourages them from applying for and sharing in opportunities for loans and farm subsidies. As reported in *Emerge* (1998), Black farmers received one-third the national average of farm subsidy payments from 1985 through 1994. Even in agriculture, we are being denied our share of the pie and may lose the little land we have.

In light of what has happened to African-American farmers, the 40 Acres and a Mule call sounds more like a desperate cry, and does more to create WDS than alleviate it. For example, *Upscale* magazine reported in 1998 that an estimated 30,000 reparations claims have been made to the IRS since 1993. Because there is no law supporting reparations to African-Americans, those who erroneously receive refunds will be required to repay the IRS. The article further states that future tax claims for reparations "will be denied on the first filing and the IRS plans to assess a $500 penalty for filing frivolous claims on those who try to file a second time."

In 1998, Congress considered an act to create a commission to study slavery's effects on African-Americans. If this was a serious attempt to understand the damage done to us in terms of our economic behavior, then the actions of 30,000 brothers and sisters filing "frivolous" claims with the IRS and voluntarily subjecting themselves to IRS scrutiny and penalty is evidence enough that our reliance on long-ago broken promises saps our energy. If this kind of activism is encouraged, we will do additional financial harm to ourselves because the focus is on government accountability, not personal accountability. Reparations, at the right time and in the right proportions are just, but cash alone in the hands of those unwilling to build a stronger community does not address the problem many of us face: Wealth Disorientation Syndrome.

We have not been persuasive in our attempts to link human with economic rights in a capitalist society. In a capitalist society, if we are not dedicated today, right now, to overthrowing and rebuilding it into something else, we must work within it. Kwame Ture (formerly Stokely Carmichael), helped us understand we are people deserving of rights, with the ability to collect on our demands for respect.

In Isabel Wilkerson's 1998 article in *Essence* entitled, "Soul Survivor," she notes that Ture, at the age of 56, has no money. Ture said of the fact that he has no money, "If you struggle for the people, the people won't let you starve." I like the thought of people struggling for others and caring for one another. Some people define the Christian and Black Radical political ideals as living communally. Communally, in this context, means collectively controlling goods and property and possessing a devotion to the group rather than society as a whole. It appears that over the last generation that individualism is the preferred way of living over communalism, but even if communalism is preferred, collectively controlling goods and property means acquisition of goods and property in order to care for one another.

According to Wilkerson's article, Ture joked with his mother that he has not given her a "penny" and has provided little financial support to his sons. Ture's belief in communalism, coupled with his inability to provide for his mother and sons is an example of the financial consequences of adhering at all costs to ideals rather than practical action where we live. I use Ture as an example because I know many sisters dream that their financial lives will be improved through communal living, however without the acquisition of wealth, there is no ability to fulfill the communal dream. We all know what happens to a "dream deferred." Langston Hughes asked if deferred dreams dry up, fester, stink, harden, sag or explode. It appears that communal dreams have at best dried up and, at worst, perpetuated the 40 acres mentality.

When influential people of all political persuasions address the issue of money, we must scrutinize their words and policy considerations carefully. We tend to agree with friends of our community, and ignore the enemies. In the popular

1970's song called, *Smiling Faces*, the group sings, "Your enemies won't do you no harm, they'll let you know where they're coming from." Former President Ronald Reagan, considered by many to be an enemy of the African-American community, told us that we cannot rely on the federal government to address our economic concerns. He told us exactly where he was coming from and still he was able to do us harm. Though forewarned, we were not economically prepared for the consequences of the financial havoc his policies wreaked.

Some will take these thoughts out of context and suggest I am an African-American who is against reparations. For the record, I am for justice. The United States, and as a consequence, most of the world, would go bankrupt if the government fully compensated us for the labor, back wages, compensatory and punitive damages, benefits, stolen property, rape, murder, and mis-education perpetrated against our ancestors. We cannot afford to push Uncle Sam into bankruptcy. What we need rests with us, and with you, taking care of our needs and wants.

In order to move ***beyond 40 acres*** — reliance on long-ago broken governmental promises that freed slaves would get 40 acres and a mule, in reparation for the damage done to slaves — ***and another pair of shoes*** — the desire to have more material possessions than we need — we have to remember and accept the harsh truths of our reality in the United States:

- ◆ Our ancestors were brought here against their will to enrich white people and build a country that has become the wealthiest nation in the world;

- ◆ We are here today to enrich others until such time we really decide we are not.

If you accept these general truths, we can move *beyond 40 acres and another pair of shoes*. If you reject outright, without question, the probability that these statements might be true, nothing will likely free you from the condition many of us endure, **Wealth Disorientation Syndrome**.

We were not given 40 acres, we will not be given 40 shares of stock. The only thing we were given is the right to participate in wealth-building institutions. Participate! We have lived as free people for over 100 years, and we have earned (and blown) enough money to participate in the market and earn the money we keep asking others to provide. We can participate right away, but it requires us to want more for ourselves and our families. I have yet to meet a sister who wants less than what she currently has. You know you want more, so let's go get it.

II. *Breaking the Chains:*

Wealth Disorientation Syndrome

5. *Wealth Disorientation Syndrome*

My clients come from a variety of ethnic and socio-economic backgrounds. I have met practically every other client through a referral from a satisfied client. I thought my client base would be as diverse as my initial clientele. I had no reason to suspect that most of the prospective clients who would refuse my services would be sisters.

I am about to run several red lights, but what I am about to say is the truth. Many sisters who have expressed an interest in improving their financial lives have agreed to meet with me, and have simply not shown up for their appointments. Many call at the last minute faking an illness. Many take weeks, if not months, to decide whether they are going to take my advice. Some have gotten angry with me when I suggested they should change what they presently do, in order to have more money. Each of these women has expressed similar fears, reservations, behaviors and attitudes about money. It is as if we all grew up in the same economically dysfunctional family.

We did not grow up in the same household, but we tend to relate to financial institutions similarly. After observing these behaviors, I detected a pattern so prevalent and now so predictable and economically destructive, that I had to identify and name it:

> ## Wealth Disorientation Syndrome (WDS)
>
> The momentary emotional imbalance during moments of personal economic decision that, if made, would ultimately lead to more wealth.

The behavior is so prevalent, profound, predictable and destructive that I felt compelled to help us talk about why we collectively have such money troubles. I hope I can help you address what may be making it difficult for you to make a decision to secure your financial life.

Let me define WDS in greater detail. When I call someone to introduce my services, I tell them that I help people make the most of their money. Building wealth is usually an attractive proposition. Everyone wants to be better off financially. If you wanted to be better off, wouldn't you naturally follow the direction toward being better off? Not if you are disoriented. Disoriented people consistently confuse left with right, up with down when it comes to choosing options for their money. These behaviors rise to the level of a syndrome when someone knowingly engages in them over and over again, realizing that she is becoming financially worse off as a result of the behavior.

If you have WDS, there is a gap in your consciousness around money. There is a gap that might be explained by our

African-American cultural expressions. If you refuse to read on, and you know you need more money, you are suffering from the worst symptom of WDS, **voluntary ignorance**. Ask yourself again and again if you really want more choices, more freedom, more security, more generosity, more dreams fulfilled, more money? Really? If the answer is yes, you must push yourself to read on. The forces of collective amnesia about our history, culture, politics and religion are all around you. You can reach from within to hear the voice that tells you that, without question, you deserve the best financial advice available, even if it hurts a little.

WDS causes one to think about unnecessary and irrelevant information in deciding whether spending money or saving and investing equals wealth. As a consequence of the dizzying effects of WDS, many of us have procrastinated on numerous wealth-building opportunities, and have therefore missed out on record-breaking wealth opportunities in the stock market. WDS results in bad timing.

WDS makes it difficult to measure the risks involved in investing. As you and your investment advisor attempt to measure the level of risks you are willing to take to arrive at your financial goals, you will probably decide not to decide. In the meantime, you go back to your old spending habits, and feed yourself messages like, "I don't make enough money to invest" or "I have things I need to purchase before I begin investing."

It may be difficult admitting to yourself that you suffer from WDS. Maybe you don't have it. If you spend too much time thinking and too little time doing anything with your money to create wealth, take a deep breath, exhale and consider the symptoms of WDS.

Symptoms of Wealth Disorientation Syndrome

- **Voluntary ignorance.** You choose not to seek or absorb information about money.

- **Procrastination.** Something more interesting or more pressing occurs almost every time you commit to dealing with your money.

- **Fear.** Your fear is informed by ignorance of financial institutions, the products they create, and the people with whom they are affiliated.

- **Half-stepping.** Because of your fear, you commit less money than you can to achieve your financial goals.

- **Back-stepping.** You began saving money regularly, then spent it all on something you didn't need.

- **Anxiety.** When it's your time to talk about your money, you feel as if time is rushing by, and your mouth can't move as fast as your thoughts.

You become nervous and lose concentration because breaking the Code of Silence is like the sound of fingernails on a chalkboard.

◆ **Dizziness**. The Code of Silence has been shattered, and you don't understand a word anyone is saying.

◆ **Nausea**. You now know the gravity of your procrastination, and realize you can't possibly pursue the dreams you had because it's too late.

Whenever we discuss important issues in a public forum, there is a concern that the messages will be misconstrued to make us look inadequate or incapable of achieving the goal. There is a concern that WDS will be perceived as pathogenic, a disease with no known cure. WDS is serious business, but it is not a disease. It is simply a metaphor that suggests that history, politics, culture, religion, and society may influence your disinterest in accumulating wealth. WDS affects how people deal with their money, but only you have power over the currency you are paid or gifted. Since you have the power, the onus is on you to become aware of the changes you need to make. For better or for worse, politics, religion, culture and society will not change at the rate you need to change in order to begin accumulating wealth today.

WDS does not have to be a persistent condition. I have seen women inarticulate in the language of money begin to talk about money and wealth building like they do about building their wardrobe. You can be transformed in a short amount of time. *Beyond 40 Acres and Another Pair of Shoes* can be your tool in the transformative process.

As time goes on, you will have opportunities to include other tools (articles, books, magazines, discussions) in your transformative process. These tools have been available to you for some time. Believe it or not, you are being bombarded with information about money. It is everywhere you are. It is on the radio, it is on television, it's on the internet, it's in the newspapers, it's in magazines, it's on the bookshelves, it surrounds you. Have you been unaware of this fact? Do you know it's true, but you tune out? If so, you may have WDS. Every time you tune out, you are making a decision to maintain your current level of awareness and understanding of money. If you have WDS, chances are you have not responded to one advertisement urging you to request additional information about a money issue. There's a good reason why this is so.

In late 1997, twenty of my African-American female clients examined advertising directed towards African-American women. The consensus was that none of the advertisements were compelling, even though they featured African-American women or were in an African-American woman's magazine. A few women said they were offended by the advertisements. Between the pictures and the words used in some ads, the group heard and inferred a rather offensive message like the following:

"Dear Welfare Queen. You've been sucking the life out of America for some time now. You blame corporate America for keeping you down, so you turn to my tax dollars to feed your illegitimate children. At ABC Financial, we understand that you are lazy, therefore we want to help you manage your money."

How have you reacted to advertisements for your money? The actual advertisements suggest that if we wanted our children to be strong and independent, then we should set an example. If you were offended, consider that financial institutions probably do not pay top dollars for full-page, color advertisements featuring African-American models with the purpose of offending their target audience. It is obvious that financial institutions by and large don't yet know how to communicate with us. However, on the two-way street of communication, there should be some point at which we say to ourselves that we are not going to deconstruct the hell out of an advertisement. If it appears in the right place, with representations of African-Americans, and offering a service we need, then seize the opportunity. There are numerous efforts afloat to attract you to financial advice and services. If you keep your eyes and ears open, you will be amazed how this information can lead you to more wealth.

6. *The Legacy Class*

Does a marketing assistant with a college degree and a salary of $25,000 put that person in the upper class of American society? What about the factory worker with no college degree making $100,000? What about entertainers who make millions of dollars? Does that make them upper-class? Many clients have told me that their parents were lower class, and therefore did not know enough about money to share advice with them. So, today, as adults, they know nothing about money.

During your childhood, no one expects you to know anything independent of your parents. Right? So why all the drama? We all know that our parents are human and therefore have their limits. For example, many of us learn about the act of sex from our parents, but the art of love-making is learned through experience, not by asking our parents. (YUCK!) By the time we are in our 30s, as many of my clients are, we are permitted to learn new things on our own and it is expected that we will.

Similarly, no one is such an "old dog" that they cannot learn "new tricks" regarding money. Your learning is hampered, however, if you blame your parents for the economic class they reared you in. Use your past as a galvanizing motivator to know more. Knowledge of financial matters has less to do with class, and more to do with:

1) Class identification,
2) The absence of a financial professional who cares about your financial well-being;
3) Wealth Disorientation Syndrome.

The only meaningful difference between you and someone in the upper financial classes is how you view your relationship with money. Middle class people know that to maintain their class position, they need to focus on ways to make the most of the money they have and expect to generate through employment. Why? People fall from middle to lower class much faster than those in the upper class. If you lost your job today, how long would it be before you needed to replace your income? If the answer is not several years, then you need to begin making the most of your money now.

To test whether you are maintaining your current economic class identification, answer the following question:

What would I do if I won $1 million?

Did you answer, "Hire a professional financial advisor or call my advisor?" If the answer is no, then chances are you identify with the lower economic classes. Your first answer (if you are wealth-building oriented) should have been something to the effect, "See if I can turn this into $1,100,000 in

12 months."

The first African-American who won a big state lottery won several million dollars, and claimed bankruptcy shortly thereafter. Recently, several African-American entertainers have filed bankruptcy. Millionaire athletes have done the same. And you are thinking, I would never do that. Right?

If you do not begin relating who you are to the value of money, you will probably be as broke as the day you won your million dollars. Why? You have given too much thought the past several years to what you don't have, but want. You have seen things unattainable to you according to your income and budget, but seemingly the same things are owned by those who look just like you and live in your neighborhood. This is the financial paradox we are living – sisters in the wealthiest nation with the highest human poverty index. You may have purchased things outside your reach because for a moment, you thought it was within your reach. Living a lower class existence in the wealthiest nation in the world is like living in a House of Mirrors – distorted images of expensive things seem as obtainable as an arm's reach, and as soon as you lunge for them, you crash into the image. You find out the hard way that most of what we perceive as real is actually an illusion.

Many well-meaning, ironically, middle class African-Americans argue that we should be entitled to the low-paying service jobs held in large part by recent immigrants. I find this view peculiar. These positions are generally low-skill, low-paying jobs. When we realize we are being exploited, we seek to get out. When stingy employers realize they cannot exploit us, they exploit others. Farm owners cannot get us to work their fields for little or no wages. We left, but the fields are still there. Who is working them now? In Sacramento, California, it is Mexican workers — the "new" slaves. These new slaves are illegal immigrants paid $56 per week in exchange for bogus immigration papers (*Oakland Tribune*, 1998).

Advocating that African-Americans should occupy low-paid, low-skill jobs, just because we fought for them and held them in greater numbers at one point in history, perpetuates the 40-acres mentality. It encourages us to identify with the lower class as a goal. If we do not reach higher, then we cannot progress. As a result of a lack of steady progression in technology, for example, U.S. employers have successfully advocated for the loosening of immigration laws to allow for the hiring of immigrants for high tech positions. As it becomes tougher to become a legal immigrant for low waged jobs, and easier for high tech jobs, there will be increased opportunities for African-Americans to return to the fields (without a concerted plan to be in high tech, or elsewhere). Let's be careful what we ask for, we may very well get it.

As we legitimately squawk about racial, sexual, and economic inequities, we must also begin equalizing ourselves by getting our financial houses in order, using tried and true methods to attain wealth. When our house is in order, and our neighbors' houses are in order, soon the neighborhood is in order. When the neighborhood is in order, schools are better, properties are worth more, and so on. We have an equal opportunity to make the most of our money. Hooray!

Let's move beyond the traditional lower, middle & upper class designations – those labels serve to distract sisters from the real issues before them such as, "what are you going to do with the money you generate?" Let's create a new class called the **Legacy Class.** We can create wealth and pass it along to the next generation if we make a promise and concerted effort. We should seriously consider entering into a social contract with the next generation to ensure their future.

I asked members of *BW2000* (2,000 Black women investing $2,000 by the year 2000) what could be different if 2,000 African-American women of financial means agreed to work together to fix a problem. They answered:

- ♦ Everything and anything we endeavor to do;

- ♦ Enhance cooperation with others to create change;

- ♦ Improve schools and after-school programs;

- ♦ Create housing for families with low incomes;

- ♦ Create stronger networks amongst African-American professionals;

- ♦ Strengthen our political voice;

- ♦ Create vocational schools;

- ♦ Open African-American universities;

- ♦ Build shopping centers in South Africa;

- Provide additional grants and scholarships;

- Hire full-time, well-paid fund raisers for Black not-for-profit organizations;

- Develop a foundation on the order of the Jewish Defense League to support working efforts to liberate our minds and develop worldwide African-based economies.

One sister responded the way many of us feel –

> I've rarely taken the opportunity to be committed to a dream/desire before. I can honestly say something within me is changing. For example, right now, there is a concert taking place in the city. I'd love to be there dancing and meeting new people, but to my surprise at the last minute, I prioritized. I want to have control of my finances. I want to save money. I want to pay back my student loans. I want to have investment consciousness. I want to live *below* my means. In the Black community, we have a need to use our resources to benefit ourselves and our community. I feel I'm making a commitment toward this change within me.

Again, many of us have not committed to a dream or desire. As someone who is in the position to hear the hopes and dreams of people from a variety of backgrounds, ethnicities and beliefs, I often hear sisters say that the reason why money is not a priority in their lives, "like it is for White people," is because we have different values. Studies suggest that our values are more similar than different. According to the U.S. Trust *Survey of Affluent Americans*, half of the survey respondents plan to leave at least some portion of their estates to:

- ◆ College or academic institution (58%)
- ◆ Health-related organizations (45%)
- ◆ Religious institutions (34%)
- ◆ Charities related to public issues like the environment or politics (24%)
- ◆ Libraries or museums (20%)

We have a rich and powerful history that no one can deny. So do the wealthy. Their ancestors were committed to a better life for them, and so were ours. As a result, many of us are earning enough money to begin investing and insuring that the next generation will be more secure and powerful than ours. Let's commit ourselves to the next generation. Our legacy will be the one of financial attainment. Let's go down in the history books as the **Legacy Class** – the first generation of African-Americans to enter into a social contract with our children committing ourselves to passing along true wealth, well-funded community institutions and a race privilege mentality.

7. Race Privilege Mentality

So much of what some sisters think about money and wealth building is connected with what we think about White people, White men in particular. We ascribe attitudes to them based on our perception of their behavior when they interact with us. Consequentially, when we attempt to bring wealth building to the top of our priority list, negative images of White men and the things they do bump wealth building off the priority list altogether. Why all the drama?

Race Privilege Mentality is the belief that one is entitled to something solely based on their race. It is something we easily identify in others, but do not positively possess ourselves. For example, imagine yourself walking down the sidewalk with the right of way. In the opposite direction comes a White individual or group of White people. You begin to wonder whether they will acknowledge your presence, and step aside so that you do not have to leave the sidewalk to continue your trek. Just as you are about to collide, you decide to step off the sidewalk. You turn around to see if they actually noticed you, but no one looks your way. That person or those people behaved rudely, and you believe they acted rudely simply because they are White, and you are not. It has happened so many times throughout your life that you cannot help but believe it has to do with some race privilege mentality they possess.

Race and racism are hyper-sensitive topics. It's draining! Please take a moment of silence to clear your thoughts of the sidewalk example. After you have cleared your head, ask yourself if you are entitled to any sort of race privilege mentality. What should you be entitled to because you are an African-American woman? Nothing, because you think people should not be entitled to anything based on race? Government assistance, because the government makes it difficult for you to get a job? Minimum wage? Social Security? Affirmative Action? What are you entitled to? You are entitled to participate in every wealth-building institution there is.

Take another moment of silence, clear your head, and imagine you have the right of way as you walk down a sidewalk full of banks and brokerage houses. Your pockets are full of cash, and your are intent on making an investment. In the opposite direction comes a group of people. Are you going to let them derail you from your purpose? Not if you understand that your privilege is to be there.

In order to foster and nurture the belief that you are entitled to participate in wealth building institutions, you may need to ignore messages from African-Americans who would accuse you of being an "Oreo" or "trying to be White" when you desire money. Further ignore the absence of messages from "White men" and financial institutions that have chosen not to talk to you about money (see the note to Financial Services Professionals) or seek your attention in advertisements. Adopt a Race Privilege Mentality to facilitate your full participation in each and every wealth-building institution in this country.

Using your privilege does not require that anyone is excluded from wealth-building institutions. Privileges can be used for positive and negative purposes. Not using the privilege is a negative act. This may sound preachy, but I believe very strongly that we have a debt to be paid to the future generation, based on the sacrifices of our ancestors to commit to building a better life for us. I doubt many sisters will disagree with me, but the level of emotion depends on how real we experience slavery.

In order to get in touch with the realities of slavery, there are two new sources: Ira Berlin's *Remembering Slavery*, an oral history told by former slaves, and *Trans-Atlantic Slave Trade, A Database on CD-ROM* produced by the W.E.B. DuBois Institute for Afro-American Research at Harvard University. Some of the facts you will find include:

- There were 27,233 slave voyages
- 11 million Africans were forced into slavery
- African slaves outnumbered free white immigrants 3-to-1

If you couple the facts with the voices of former slaves recalling the barbarity of their treatment, you will understand that our moral duty is to adopt a race privilege mentality toward wealth and a better life for our future. A better life does not mean conspicuous consumption, i.e. buying everything our forebears could not. If you are spending beyond your means, you may be justifying your actions with a negative sense of a Race Privilege Mentality. Spending beyond your means is the perpetuation of spiritual poverty. You have lost awareness. Without spirit, you cannot see that most of what you really need, you already have. If you are spending beyond your means, lower your expenses, and accept that all you really need materially, you already have. This is not what most people see as deprivation, this is abundance in its various forms. If you have WDS, you have already deprived yourself of wealth.

You do not have a race privilege mentality entitlement to future poverty, but no one will block your way on the sidewalk if your goal is to shop until you drop. Therefore, tell yourself when you are in your favorite department store:

Every time I'm in here, I contribute to their wealth. They have done nothing to contribute to my wealth, and I have done nothing to contribute to my own wealth. I work hard, and I deserve more than this pair of shoes. I have been deprived of their profits.

As soon as this realization, awareness, and awakening of your inner spirit happens, walk out of the store. It won't be easy to walk out, especially since you just walked in, and the sales person comes after you. Again, reach deep inside yourself to hear the voice of discipline, moral obligation to the future, and abundance in its various forms.

We have been known to respect (and fear) discipline. Discipline is a virtue that separates the truly successful from the failures. Adopting a Race Privilege Mentality is a step in treating Wealth Disorientation Syndrome. When WDS is eliminated, you have created in your life the recipe for financial success.

Are you ready to receive your new attitude? Can you hear the voice of discipline? Are you ready to be privileged? Do you have a duty toward the success of others? If so, your privilege is ownership of institutions, not ownership of what they produce. Anyone can do the conspicuous consumption/buying gig. People are only superficially and temporarily impressed by what you have purchased, but no one is substantively impressed, not even yourself. Your privilege is ownership in Gucci, for example, not the shoes they manufacture. Anyone can wear new shoes. Big deal! If you want to impress your sister, talk to her about your investment portfolio. Tell her you are *entitled* to own stock and when the company doesn't perform, you are *entitled* to take your money elsewhere. That's the new mental attitude. Wear it well!

8. *The Black Working Woman and Love*

The African-American Working Woman. The description brings to mind a logic exam I took for law school: If a woman works, is she African-American? If a woman is African-American, is she a working woman? Are all working women African-American or do all African-American women work?

Do you know many African-American women who are capable of working, but have never held a job? They do exist, and the popular mass media would make us think it is the norm. However, our collective reality does not agree with the image of the *non-working* African-American woman who has no financial cares, except her next welfare check. We were brought here to enrich others through slave labor. For over 200 years, we worked the fields, worked the "Big House," reproduced and fed slave babies. In this century we were Mammies to White babies and housekeepers and cleaners to their mothers.

This phenomenal period of human degradation has left its mark on us in how we relate to economic freedom: we work very, very hard to have more money to spend. Many of us work overtime, or have two jobs, in order to generate more income. Some of us work like crazy because of the influence of the financial paradox: "if it appears that most people can have the things I think I need to live comfortably, I am willing to generate enough income through work to make those purchases." Many of us work one job that requires 12 – 15 hours a day, leaving no time for quiet time, family time, pursuit of happiness time, or time to find and nurture the love we want in a mate. Because we work and work to the point of exhaustion, to the point of neglect of other aspects of our lives, we often become aware that there is no wealth to show for our years of hard work. Working does not equal wealth, even if you have a guaranteed job for life.

In the 1997 financial disclosures for U.S. Supreme Court justices, Justice Ruth Bader Ginsburg, reported that her net worth was somewhere between $5.9 and $24.1 million, *up* from $4.9 to $15.4 million in one year. Justice Clarence Thomas reported $30,000 to $175,000, *down* from $80,000 to $275,000 in one year. Justice Thomas has been on the bench longer than Justice Ginsburg. Justice Thomas is getting poorer as he works. Working does not necessarily equal wealth. (*San Francisco Chronicle*, 1998)

You are working hard with little to show for it. If you go home to no one, perhaps you dream that life would be much simpler if you were married to someone who has money. Why do we dream of financial independence in a mate, and not in ourselves? And why do we dream we can be attractive to someone with money if we have no money? What does it really mean to be taken care of?

Let's say you are in a steady relationship (married or otherwise) with someone. Your mate takes care of the bills, because you do not want to. You are relieved, right? Don't be relieved, be frightened.

I advised a 50-year old woman who was in her tenth year of marriage. She needed a lot of hand-holding (which I am happy to do) because she had not made a significant financial decision in a decade. For the last decade she had handed her paycheck to her husband, who takes care of the bills. Though employed, she had managed to save only $1,200, or $120 a year. Her salary was $54,000 from a full time job. She knew nothing about her husband's assets or liabilities or any joint ownership arrangements. The frightening truth is that if her husband predeceases her, she will be responsible for his debts and obligations. Is this comforting? Is acquiescence to spousal control worth it in the end?

You need to ask your mate to show you (not tell you) what is in place for your present and future financial plans. It may be difficult, especially if you've been together for some time, and you have never asked the question before. You may arouse suspicion if you take the direct approach (but some people prefer directness). If your spouse responds favorably to indirectness, imagine this setting:

You're at home on the evening of pay day. The lights are low (but not too low as to be seductive) and the music is turned on low (but upbeat and instrumental only to create the mood of relaxation and optimism). You prepare a quick and hearty meal that generates the aroma of richness (somehow fried bologna does not come to mind). You pour full-bodied red wine (none of that blush stuff) into large wine glasses, and ask your mate to smell the wine, several times. You turn the music up a notch after each whiff and as you do so, the aroma of the food wafts around your mate's head. You return to the kitchen and bring the food into the room. By now, your mate is ready to ask why you are behaving as you are. You simply say that today is pay day, that you are very grateful that the two of you have made it this far, and you want to honor the success of your relationship. You clink your wine glasses in a toast, for your mate is in perfect agreement. You acknowledge that one of the reasons why you feel fortunate is because your mate is still alive, well, and able to enhance your life. Should they predecease you, everything will be different, and you will not know what to do. Your mate will probably assure you that you will be fine. At this point all you have to do is ask that on the evening of the next pay day, that you have dinner again, with wine and music and the details of your current financial lives. Your loving mate will probably agree.

If your mate refuses, your relationship is more about control. If you are working, you need to have joint control, if not total control over your finances. Some sisters are in relationships where no one seems capable of handling their finances individually, let alone collectively. If this is true for you and your spouse, seek out the advice of a financial advisor who works with couples.

Many of us would like our relationships to be different than they are. We want someone to take care of us and deal with the things we do not like dealing with (especially finances). It is reasonable to feel this way because we are probably the most neglected group of people in this country. Feeling neglected, and relying on our mates who show love through control, it is no wonder that so many of us who survive our mates have no knowledge of their financial affairs.

Forty acres is a dream. Happily marrying rich is the same kind of dream that can postpone the initiative to examine critically what you do with your own money. Dreaming, and not doing, also clouds the reality about marriages in today's society — over 50% of marriages end in divorce. More women are in the work force, and getting less and less in alimony and child support.

We want love and money, i.e., a lover with money willing to share it. Separate the need for love from the need to be taken care of financially and you will discover this: Money can't buy you love, but money can "buy" you more money. You work for money, not for love. Use the money you earn to accumulate the wealth you would like your ideal lover to provide. When you become more financially sound, your concern about what others will provide will dissipate. Eventually, you will be more attractive to those with money because you will begin doing things with your money that wealthy people do. As a consequence, you will begin talking about money. When we break the Code of Silence, people will begin to open up to you. Perhaps sooner than you think, you may find the love you are looking for, not because *they* have money, but because *you* already have the money you need.

9. *Plastic Crack*

By now you have heard the theory that our communities are infested with drug addicts because the government introduced drugs into our communities. Whether you believe this theory or not, there has been another type of drug responsible for the economic destruction in our communities. This drug is ***Plastic Crack***, a.k.a. credit cards. Financial institutions have infested our non-working family, friends, and neighbors with *plastic crack* to increase their bottom-line.

Why would a financial institution send an unsolicited "pre-approved" credit card application to someone who is not working? Someone who has never worked? Someone who is in high school, on his or her way to college and therefore not in a position to work for another four years? Someone with poor credit? By and large, credit cards are addictive to those who have unattainable material wants, and the financial institutions profit from these desires. It is unethical to make profits in this way. It is the reason why many of us who make decent salaries cannot invest for wealth. Our lives are ruled by repaying the financial institutions that introduced plastic crack into our homes.

Let's examine their methods.

PRE-APPROVED!

No security deposit required
Frequent credit line increases
You are pre-approved for a credit line up to ...

Dear Ms. Minimum Payment:

You know how important it is to have a credit card — and a good credit history — in today's world. A credit card lets you face emergency expenses without worry or carrying extra cash...order goods over the phone...rent a car or make travel reservations...even get cash instantly.

You are already approved! Send no money with this Acceptance certificate! At ABC Bank, we believe consumers like you should have access to the convenience and purchasing power of a ABC credit card without sending a security deposit. That's why you've been selected to receive this special pre-approved unsecured... offer. Whether you use your ABC Bank card...to shop, dine, or just for emergencies, you'll feel confident knowing your card will be accepted at over 13 million locations worldwide! And, you can obtain cash advances at over 257,000 locations around the world...

Three billion letters like this one were sent in 1997 according to the Consumer Federation of America. Three billion?! Imagine billions of people, some of them too young and inexperienced to know that money does not grow on trees, getting letters that promise shopping, dining, and spending in millions of locations throughout the world. These letters offer convenience, material goods, travel and even "instant cash." To the unsuspecting, these words offer us prestige, a way out, a feel-good escape. Crack, and its peddlers, offer the same thing.

For some of us who accept these offers of an instant high, we have momentary feelings of power. Then, our material possessions and "instant cash" turn on us. What we thought we needed and had to have immediately, are now the last things we need. The dope we took no longer makes us feel good, we feel awful. To feel better, we need more dope. To feel better, we need more money to pay for the "instant cash," the instant high. We begin looking for a way out. There is no easy way. We begin to cry for help. No one can really help without exacting a huge cost. We begin to regret we ever accepted the offer. No one likes to live with regrets.

It is ironic that so many of us are in debt, when culturally, we have a strong bias against owing others money. Our culture was to pay cash for what we wanted and needed. We used to pay outright, and when we did not have the money, we did not get the desired object (or we put it on lay-away). Our culture has gone from paying cash outright, to paying nothing in large part because financial institutions introduced credit cards to the financially vulnerable and immature in our communities. Imagine the possibilities if financial institutions introduced stock market investing into our communities. Hmmm? We might be wealthier if they did. In the meantime, we need to eradicate from our families and neighborhoods, the one drug that keeps people legally liable to corporate America — credit card debt.

How do you determine whether you are addicted or prone to be addicted to plastic crack? It is very easy. Let's begin with the assumption that an addict has a credit card balance that cannot be paid with discretionary income next month. Carrying a debt balance with interest, how often do you stop to think about how changes in our economy can affect you? If you use credit cards, carry a revolving balance, and never seriously ponder the above question, you are addicted. Your credit card abuse does not change as the economy changes because you are so high on the use that you do not think rationally about the fluctuations in interest rates and changes in the economy.

Consumer confidence usually refers to how secure people feel about their ability to survive in a dynamic economy. If you are not confident about your ability to extinguish your credit card debt the following month, you should reduce your debt and begin to save money. If after comparing balances, you see that you have less saved than borrowed, and you continue to use your credit card , then you are addicted.

If you seriously ponder the question of consumer confidence, and determine that you can purchase unnecessary items with cash, but prefer the use of your credit (and don't pay your balance off the next month), you are probably addicted. Some of my clients have argued that they are lazy about paying bills. We have all heard that after the high, drugs make you feel lazy. Others have said that they are reestablishing their credit. The best way to do that is to pay off your balance, not just pay the minimum required.

Overall, plastic crack, like powdered crack, as I understand it, makes you feel like you are something you are not.

Powdered Crack	*Plastic Crack*
You feel invincible.	You feel you can walk into a store, where everyone else has to pay, but you get to take things for free!
Leaves you wanting more	Possessing material goods without the cash to pay for it, leaves you wanting more because you possess something you did not work for.
"It's recreational. I'm not addicted."	"It's recreational. I'm not addicted."
As your tolerance builds, you need more and more to get a high.	As the higher credit limit raises your tastes upward, it costs more to satisfy you. The more expensive must be better.
"I only use it when I need to feel happier."	"It's just for emergencies."

Plastic crack credit cards are more tools of economic destruction for the holder, than they are means for financial management.

Plastic Crack Detox

If you have department store credit cards, and a major credit card, begin plastic crack detox by closing your department store accounts. You do not need them, the interest rates are highway robbery, and they keep you in the 40 acres and another pair of shoes mentality.

If you know drug addicts, then you know they are often in denial about their level of addiction. Are you in denial about your dependency on credit cards? It might be better to ask someone who knows you well. If you have more credit card debt than you can extinguish in a month's time, use plastic crack detox by cutting up your cards, and phoning the credit institutions to close your accounts. If you have a few thousand dollars of debt, your time in detox will be shorter. If you have several thousand dollars or more, with an inability to pay your bills, you need intense detoxification.

Do you know converts? Converts are people who have successfully gone through a recovery program. Converts lived a life of misery because they had no control over what hurt them the most. They then turned themselves around and are now the happiest, most enthusiastic, disciplined people you know. One day, you will feel the same way.

First, you must feel the anger. If you are addicted to plastic crack, you should be angry with the financial institutions who introduced you to crack, and angry with yourself for not going through detox sooner. Second, you should seek to have some control over how they do business with our communities. You should want to be more in control of what goes on. Control cannot be had if there is no ownership of anything. When you are in the position to invest, you will be in a control position. Until such time, you must go through the fire and detox your system of plastic crack. You may feel like you are on fire, but once the flames are extinguished, you will come out converted, ready to invest, and in control — but only if you win the war.

You have heard about the war on drugs. Congress is now plotting another war, on consumer debtors. With a 21% increase (1.35 million filings) in personal bankruptcies from 1996 to 1997, Congress is attempting to make it more difficult for people to successfully file for bankruptcy. When Congress wages wars against individuals and not the institutions that create the problem, we know they will lose the war.

The problem is not the ease with which people can buy drugs. The problem is not the ease in which people can file bankruptcy. The issue is the creation of the need for something that looks good on its face, but is ultimately destructive. For a financial institution to encourage financially-immature or financially-irresponsible people to buy on credit is like a dope dealer encouraging an unhappy person to find happiness through drugs. Creditors, like other financial service providers, should take an ethical approach to what they are doing in poorer communities and the potentially wealthy communities presently on college campuses. One idea is to offer cards with a lower interest rate (4 percent) that can only be used for food, shelter, and books. Why should young people who are not work-who are not working pay high interest rates? If it is not feasible for creditors to lower rates for young people, it is not feasible for them to offer the card.

Let the solution begin institutionally. Rather than targeting young people and people with past credit problems, banks should publicize information about their savings and investing programs. It is that simple.

10. *Financial Hopscotch and the Teeter Totter Effect*

Now that you have been reminded of the fact, accept the truth: you are entitled to participate in this country's riches by virtue of the fact that our ancestors invested in your right to do so. If you have some money to invest, but you have done nothing about it, it may be because you have a love-hate relationship with American institutions.

The U.S. is the country many of us love to hate. We rarely talk affectionately about the "home of the free and the brave," because, generally speaking, we neither love nor hate it. We have a ***Nationality Ambivalence***, and understandably so. We have gone through the metamorphosis of being colored, Negro, Black, Black American, and African American. Only recently have we permitted ourselves to call ourselves American, but we have not discussed whether we feel differently about our adopted country.

Our nationality ambivalence tends to be the reason we do not participate in the institutions we identify as American (recall the definition of popular capitalism) at their core. When we couple our ambivalence with the U.S. with notions of an allegiance to the motherland Africa, we become apathetic, showing little or no interest in what is going on here as it relates to our economy. We react to racism because we know its effects; we do not react to swings in the economy because we think it doesn't affect us. This kind of apathy is the same kind of apathy that discourages us from voting. Nationality Ambivalence leads to a lack of participation in institutions that could benefit us when utilized.

It is no wonder that we have so much ambivalence toward this country. We constitute one of the most maligned groups of people in the history of the country. Brought here in chains, in ships, in slavery, raped, separated from loved ones, freed, lied to, hired for slave wages, discriminated against, we are also blamed for the economic woes of America. As a consequence, we initially tend to avoid things that are American at their core (when was the last time you said the Pledge of Allegiance with conviction?)

Institutions that are American at their core are those that deal with money. Too many of us avoid them, to our detriment. In avoiding them, we play the game of *Financial Hopscotch.*

Financial Hopscotch

Financial Hopscotch is played similarly to the hopscotch you played as a child. As a child, you threw a rock on a square, then jumped onto the square with the hope of avoiding the lines dividing the squares. Financial Hopscotch, played under the rules of nationality ambivalence, is played by throwing money or hopes onto the green thin lines separating you from real wealth, located inside the squares. The lines are green because that is where most of your extra money is. You avoid the squares because that is where your ambivalence lies. The green lines represent where we often find our discretionary money: credit card companies, friends and family, church (*aspiritual* tithing is discussed in another section), department stores and passport savings accounts (when your objective is growth and/or income). The squares represent vehicles for financial wealth and security.

In an effort to make typically boring information less intimidating, I have defined different financial vehicles used for income and growth.

♦ **Long-term care insurance**. This is what you need before you become old, ugly, bossy and unable to care for yourself. It allows you to afford to hire others to take care of you, and may save you and your children from having to live together the rest of your lives. It may also protect your assets from being liquidated (so you can pass them along to your loved ones).

♦ **Mutual funds**. You just left the shoe store knowing that you deserve to be one of the owners, but you are wondering how profitable the company is. Then you think about all the other shoe manufacturers making money. You think you do not have enough money to invest in all the shoe companies there are, but even if you did, you do not have time to track the success or failure of each company. The ideal situation is to put your money in a "pool" with other people, spread it out between several companies, and hire a professional to manage the money.

♦ **Bonds**. You know how some people use credit cards to advance an immediate and particular need? Sometimes companies have immediate and particular needs, and need someone to loan them money. If you loan them money, they give you a bond and a promise to give you a certain return (thanks for letting us borrow your money) in a certain number of years. You know how you have paid your creditors extra for the convenience of borrowing money? Now you can be a creditor to a company, and they are obligated to pay you!

♦ **Money Market Instruments**. Sometimes people need your cash to conduct their business, and sometimes they will pay you a little for the convenience of using your money to make a transaction. Money is exchanged between financial institutions for borrowers, and they have to get the cash from somewhere. If you put your money in a money market fund, it is invested in highly liquid investments, and you get a little interest on your deposit.

♦ **Life Insurance**. People say African-American babies are born into families with no real wealth because we do not pass along money. A person of little means can create an immediate estate by having life insurance. That person pays something every month, and the insurance company has to pay another person (the beneficiary) lots of money when that person dies. A person who has $30 a month might be able to pass along $500,000 to their loved ones after they are gone.

♦ **Real Property**. This refers to real estate buildings and land, such as your personal residence. For many people, their home is the largest investment they'll make in a lifetime. But it shouldn't be the only one.

♦ **Annuities**. These are the income generators you might need if you live a long time past your income-producing years. It beats relying on Social Security for periodic income after retirement.

♦ **Disability Insurance**. Your greatest asset is your ability to generate income, but if you become sick or injured to the point you can't work, it pays you a percentage of your salary.

♦ **Passport Savings**. Your money is in a plain old savings account at the bank earning 1-2% if you are lucky. Taking 3-4% inflation into account, you will have less "real" money in the bank same time next year.

The above is what you might find in the squares of your Financial Hopscotch board. Think about your financial goals and the fact that you are not near achieving them. Are you giving your money to credit card companies, family and friends, church and department stores, because you are obligated to do so by law, by relationships, by religion and by the desire to look good? What investment returns have you received by playing the game this way? Many people play this way, because the emotional return is high. However, the objective of Financial Hopscotch should be to land not on the thin green lines, but to land firmly on the squares of mutual funds, bonds, money market instruments, annuities, life insurance, stocks, disability insurance, bonds, health insurance, and real property. Time your moves to land only when the rules of the game call for your being in that particular square.

How are you going to play to win Financial Hopscotch if you suffer from a Nationality Ambivalence? Answer these two questions:

1) Colored, Negro, Black, Black American or African-American, do you plan to live in the U.S. the rest of your life?

2) Is the U.S. in the next several years, going to be anything else but capitalistic?

If you answered yes and no respectively, you are on your way to winning Financial Hopscotch. To play to win, do not simply accept that you have a Nationality Ambivalence. Remove the ambivalence by accepting the fact that the U.S. has the strongest economy in the world (despite the fact that it has the highest human poverty index of the industrialized nations). Ambivalence is an obstacle to your participation in the wealth building institutions we helped create.

You are now ready to begin playing to win. So, here are the rules.

The Rules

1) **Redefine what monetary power means to you.** Some people give lots of money to politicians with the hope they are buying power. Some people give to a charity to be invited onto the board of directors. Some people buy what they absolutely do not need because they feel they are powerless everywhere else but a department store. If you feel that you exercise your monetary power by buying and spending, then you are about to lose the game again. Monetary power means the ability to care for yourself without working.

2) **Repeat the "Saving Mantra."** Every time you get paid, say to yourself, "I can invest and save whatever I want, whenever I want, which leaves me very little to spend frivolously." Again, "I can invest and save whatever I want, whenever I want, which leaves me very little to spend frivolously." Aloud now, "I can invest and save whatever I want, whenever I want because I am entitled to own a piece of someone's corporation." If you say this to yourself every time you get paid, and actually play the game to win, you will win (and have fun playing as well).

3) **Map out your strategy**. Your biggest most formidable opponent is your ambivalence. Identify your other weaknesses, if you have them, and attack them. If you are not objective enough to do this, consult an advisor.

4) **Determine how much you spend on extras monthly**. This is the amount you will have available to save and invest.

5) **Label that money, "FOR ME."** This is the money you are going to begin skillfully throwing onto the squares.

6) **Decide what you would like to have happen in your life**, not for tomorrow, but five, ten, fifteen years from now. Depending on how old you are, do not stop at fifteen. Decide how you want to live thirty years from now. Remember, you can be your own worst enemy. Inside most of us is a voice telling us what we

can't do. This voice receives support in the popular press, so you must constantly listen to your positive voice.

7) **Play the game, over and over again**. The more you play, the better you will become.

8) **Choose your Financial Hopscotch playmates with care**. Determine who, in your life, are financial winners. Count the people in your life, who have influence and money. Have you seen their investment portfolios? Do they talk about how much their investments have grown? Did they tell you how long it took before their investment appreciated 10%, 15%, 20% or more? Did they tell you about the losses? Were they short-term or long-term? Did they stay in the market, or get out quickly? Use your financial advisor as a coach. Each successful game player has a strategy for winning. Your advisor will help you devise your winning strategy.

9) **Put learning the game at the top of your priority list**. If you are a smart sister who thinks too much and does too little about her money, your strategy for winning will not be the same year after year. Remember, the more you play, the better you will be. Don't wait to learn the game as you near the end of your income-producing years. Begin now because you do not know when your income-producing years will end.

When you run a race against others, the rules require you to start at the same place, and start at the same time with the command, "On your marks, ready, set, go!" People who *intend* to win leave the blocks immediately, but people who merely *want* to win, leave the blocks after they've thought about whether they can win. As you begin to question whether you intend to win, or simply want to win, you experience the ***teeter totter effect***. Financial planning moves to the top of your priority list, then down the list, then up the list, then down the list. Before you know it, you have procrastinated, and lost the race. The teeter totter effect is best illustrated with an example.

A woman took the initiative to call me requesting a meeting immediately because the IRS was about to garnish her wages. Because she was in trouble, financial planning was suddenly at the top of her priority list. We met, and I advised her that she would have to reduce her unnecessary expenses, write the IRS, and offer to pay them a portion of her discretionary amount to avoid garnishment. Weeks later, she had not written the letter. Financial planning had dropped to the bottom of her list because she had to make major lifestyle changes.

Shortly thereafter, the IRS began garnishing her wages. Financial planning rose to the top, again. She called me, and I referred her to a tax attorney. Weeks later, she called me back because she had misplaced the attorney's telephone number. Financial planning had fallen back down the list.

Her ride on the **teeter totter** delayed her actions, thereby creating a situation that could have been avoided. It did not help that she had to deal with the IRS, another institution we love to hate.

If you have a nationality ambivalence toward financial institutions, but you want to succeed financially, you do not have to sell-out to buy-in, nor do you have to pledge your allegiance to the flag. You must pledge allegiance to yourself, no matter what country you live in, no matter how you identify yourself. We all need shelter, we all need food, whether we are working, or not. Pledge to yourself that you will always have what you need, even if you cannot work for it. If you do not, then pray that God will bless you with the ability to work the rest of your life because working the rest of your life is the only alternative to winning Financial Hopscotch.

11. *Reclaiming the Word "Ownership"*

We often say that the economic problems in the African-American community stem from the lack of ownership and patronage of African-American-owned businesses. Without full integration in which cash flows to and from other communities into our own, owning Black businesses is not enough. We should also own other people's businesses. What? You read it right! Own something that we did not create? Why not!? If you have the proper race privilege mentality, you will become an owner in companies built by others. Yet, even though we speak the "we should own" rhetoric, we have not addressed the issue of ownership, and what it means as African-Americans.

Ownership is a loaded concept for us because our ancestors were owned, as tradable property, by Whites. Our ancestors were traded in the slave market. Puny, sickly, elderly slaves did not trade as heavily as young and strong slaves. If you were a slave trader, you would probably profit more from the slave who could work more, and would work many years. The same evaluation that went into valuing slaves, is the same valuation that pertains to valuing corporations. If you want to buy stocks (ownership in corporations), buy what you think will last a long time, and prove to be a strong contender for making profits. Whether we feel comfortable with this or not, it is the same mindset the slave owners had about our people. We must adopt the same mindset of determining profitability, but applying it to corporations, not people.

Politically speaking (from the far left), the assertion that African-Americans should have a race privilege mentality and become owners in corporate America is repugnant if you think about the exploitation of people for profits. Many have said that they refuse to invest because it helps corporations exploit others. On the other hand, we are big on having the American Dream, a "home" (approximately 45% of African-Americans own homes). How is it that we strive for the American Dream but shun the best opportunities for wealth in this country? It is the 40 acres and a mule mentality. Home ownership does not fully advance the economic agenda of the Black community, but it is a start.

Profitable ownership of a corporation is the best position you can be in to determine your financial destiny. If profitable ownership gives you the right to make decisions, then you need to be an owner of something profitable. Invest in profitable companies. You are entitled to be an owner because your Race Privilege Mentality informs you that in the absence of reparations long ago, you must seize the wealth opportunities presented to you. These opportunities are presented daily in newspapers, magazines, books, and with financial professionals. If you have the ability to invest, and have not saved, invested or insured, you may have wealth disorientation syndrome as to where the wealth is, or Nationality Ambivalence may be the obstacle to your taking ownership. People tend to care more about what they own rather than what they rent. Many of us act as if we are renters of American soil. As a result, we don't own our portion of America.

I once advised a woman who thought that if she invested more money, she would be ineligible for governmental benefits if she needed it. As some sisters think, this woman thought that if she poorly invested and saved for herself, the federal government would subsidize her living standard. She was wrong. Please understand that we must stop and smell the money. Money is not generated by the federal government, it is generated by Corporate America. You are entitled to these profits by owning their stock (you are also entitled to the losses when the stocks decrease in value).

Orient yourself toward corporate ownership. As you are orienting yourself toward corporate ownership, and becoming a corporate owner, do not be disoriented from this goal if the stock market is down. If it is down, talk to your advisor about bargain investing. Use your skills of waiting for the "One-Day Sale" to buy for less. You may be able to invest in great companies for less!

III. *On the Path to Wealth*

12. *What's An Investment?*

Buying Shoes and The Stock Market

I love shoes, don't you? I remember the time when I must have had about 15 pairs, and my friends told me I was just a novice! I had black shoes, brown shoes, red flats, purple spikes, and shoes for every sport. Sandals that covered my toes, mules, clogs, thongs, earth shoes, and biking shoes. I wore snow boots, rain boots, cowboy boots, hiking boots, and go-go boots. I also had house slippers. Shoes are a fashion statement, and a status symbol depending on the designer. I know I am not alone in my appreciation for shoes. My mother had many shoes, and so did her mother. When I go to a department store, I enjoy watching women model shoes they might possibly buy, and probably don't need. Given all the time we have put into shopping for shoes, wouldn't you think we could identify good buys for just about anything, including stocks?

Social psychologists have studied individual economic behavior, and what they have concluded is fascinating. In answering the question, "Why do people buy what they do?"

they concluded that we buy what will give us maximum use or utility, *and* we buy as an expressive function of consumption (*The Individual in the Economy*, S.E.G. Leas, R. M. Tarpy and P. Webley). If this is true, then most of the time we are buying for the expression of consumption. Theoretically, stocks provide maximum utility over another pair of shoes, so why do we prefer to express consumption over utility?

George Katona, an economic psychologist, studied the tendency to buy by asking people how they felt about the state of the economy. If they responded that they thought the economy would remain stable or improve, it followed that they expressed a certain confidence that they could easily purchase the things they wanted to buy. Most of my clients who have issues around spending too much are not concerned about the state of the economy. They are concerned about the state of their immediate gratification.

According to psychologists, the opposite of spending is saving. Katona suggests that there are two types of saving, contractual and discretionary. Contractual is the automatic deduction from one's paycheck into their 401(k), or the automatic debit from one's checking account into their mutual funds. Discretionary saving involves an active decision to save during a particular period of time. Discretionary saving (the opposite of discretionary buying) concerns us most.

Discretionary saving usually does not happen as often as it should. When we spend rather than save or invest, we miss another opportunity to learn what we could do with our money. Every month, another missed opportunity. Every year, 12 opportunities, *gone*. After 10 years of working and spending, 120 monthly opportunities to learn about saving and investing, *gone*. After 20 years of working and spending, 240 missed opportunities. It is no wonder many of us say,

I know absolutely nothing about the stock market.

For those of you who believe you know absolutely nothing about it, everything you really need to know, right now, is contained in the next few paragraphs. If you hesitate to read on, you are suffering from the worst symptom of WDS, *voluntary ignorance*. If you refuse to read and understand the next few paragraphs, you may never achieve wealth the tried and true way, in the stock market. Take time, right now, to reorient yourself from the dizzying effects of WDS. Fight the internal voice that may be screaming, "I know nothing about the stock market. I don't want to know anything about it!" Now tell yourself,

I really want more choices, more freedom, more security, more generosity, and more money.

Just to be on the safe side, say it aloud:

I really want more choices, more freedom, more security, more generosity, and more money.

You are now ready to continue reading uninterrupted by the negative messages you have been feeding yourself for the past several years.

Imagine you are in a department store and you are there to buy a pair of shoes. You walk to the women's shoe section where you have a choice of shoes from various designers and manufacturers — Aigner, Bandolino, Bass, Birkenstock, Cole-Hahn, DKNY, Easy Spirit, Ferragamo, Gucci, Kinney's, Nickels, Timberland. Some shoes have leather uppers and soles, some have rubber soles, some are lace ups, others have buckles, some soles are stitched, the others glued. Your budget for a pair of shoes is no more than $150 (but you know that if you catch a good sale, you'll get the same pair for $75). Your years of experience help you to determine a good bargain and the going rate for a good pair of shoes.

Shoe designers know there are people like you willing to pay $150 for the comfort or style of particular shoes, therefore they make sure their shoes are available in the department store for your consumption. The shoe designers are vying for your $150, all in one place. The shoe designers have created a *market* at the department store, and whichever shoes you choose, the designer (and those involved in bringing the shoes into the market) receives your $150. In exchange for your $150, you get a pair of shoes. The designer gets $140 because the shoes only cost ten dollars to produce. Who is better off in the transaction?

The department store, the middlemen, the manufacturer, and the designer have your money and the millions of dollars spent by others. You are left with another pair of shoes you did not need. The profits (when there are such) are then distributed (at the discretion of the board of directors) to those who invested in the company. You own another pair of shoes, but you do not own a part of the company. The best position for you, in relation to that company, is to be an owner of that company. The best position for your financial growth is to own a piece of the company. A piece of that company is called *stock*. Have you heard the phrase to "take stock" in something? It means ownership. If you can own shoes, you can be an owner in a corporation.

All you need to know about the stock (ownership in a corporation) market (places to buy ownership) is that you shop and buy in the stock market, just like you shop and buy in the shoe section of the department store. Now you need someone to help you shop, just like the salesperson in the store.

While you are shopping in the department store of corporate ownership, your investment advisor will help you determine the best investment fit for you. When you tell the shoe salesperson what you want, they will ask you what you want to achieve. Are you looking for comfort, style, or a combination thereof? Your investment advisor will ask you about your objectives. Do you want comfort or style? Do you want something that will last a long time? Are you looking for something flashy? Maybe you like the classic look. You know enough about shopping for value (leather lasts longer than fabric), and bargain shopping (buying when the price is low), and selling (do so when people will spend more than you paid) to know that with a little advice, you can begin buying into wealth.

People need, and pay companies for the food, shelter, clothing, energy, water, and technology those companies bring to the market of investors. You know this is true because you pay for these things yourself. There are millions of people spending money in millions of places. Would you like to profit from it? **Take your shoe budget from last year, and apply it to this year's investment budget.** You are more ready than you think to move beyond another pair of shoes.

Basic Investment Objectives

Let's keep this real simple. There are only two basic money-making investment objectives: *growth and income*. The growth objective means you invest in opportunities when it appears from research on a company's financial health that their stock price will grow in value. Growth can be achieved aggressively, moderately, and/or internationally.

Generally speaking, the income category is for people who want just enough return to provide a consistent and predictable amount of money. Many African-American women identify with this objective because it sounds guaranteed, but it is not. One would think that with only two basic investment objectives, we could choose one that will allow us more money.

Unfortunately, we often choose a third objective that provides stagnation — capital preservation, which preserves the value of the money set aside.

African-Americans have traditionally been preservation-oriented. Whites have shown themselves to be growth-oriented. Women invest more in preservation, while men invest in growth. In summary, white men (growth) earn more on their money than African-American women (preservation).

Neither your gender nor your race alone determines your investment objective. One reason why we invest conservatively is because our nationality ambivalence leads to apathy. For instance, many of us do not vote, and many of us do not invest aggressively. Voting, like investing, means we believe something good will happen as a result of it. Investing aggressively requires a belief that some company or companies, and therefore the nation, will grow and be better off. We have not vested, figuratively, and therefore are not vested literally in the growth of this nation. To be vested means a potential for growth of our money. I want us to have more money, ambivalent or not.

Your advisor should help you free your mind so that you become less ambivalent and less apathetic in order to make good financial choices. You can and must become growth oriented. Remember, we are the Legacy Class. In order to pass along wealth, we have to generate it. Someone once gave me this piece of advice that is so simple and right, it is too profound to keep to myself.

The secret to getting ahead, is getting started.

13. *Procrastination, Procrastination: It's Making Me Broke, Broke, Broke*

Do you consider yourself an analytical person? When you are hungry, and standing in front of a familiar and afford-able restaurant, do you ask yourself:

> **Well, just how hungry am I? When did I last eat? What did I last eat? Was there enough nutrition to carry me through to the next meal? Am I Vitamin-D deficient? Am I eating for comfort or because I am bored?**

If you take yourself through this before meals, you are either *analytical* (you actually possess the information nec-essary to make the correct decision) or you are *overthinking* (putting yourself through unnecessary mental exercises and procrastinating in making a decision.)

Ask yourself this question and write down your answer:

> **Do I want more money?**

In coming up with your answer did you think: where will I get it, when can I expect to get more, who will give it to me, and how can I really get more with this job I have today? Chances are you did not overthink the answer to the question; "Do I want more money?" The answer was *yes*, without hesitation.

Many of my African-American female clients overthink the wealth opportunities I present to them. They are not analyzing, they are overthinking. The difference between analyzing and overthinking is that analysis can only be achieved with the proper standards of evaluation. Many of us do not have the standards, and are not going to do the independent research necessary to make an informed decision. Why?

Wealth Disorientation Syndrome (WDS): the momentary emotional imbalance during moments of personal economic decision, that if made, would ultimately lead to wealth. WDS causes one to think about unnecessary and irrelevant information in deciding whether spending money or saving and investing equals wealth.

I met with a woman who had met with an advisor from my firm several years before our first meeting. Her first advisor suggested options that went unheeded. Several years later, she was in a worse financial position, having grown older without any investments. Recognizing she was worse off, she wanted to begin planning again. Her current lifestyle allowed only $100 monthly: her car payment was over $400 monthly; she had nothing in savings, and no mid-term investments. She contributed very little to her 401(k) plan.

Of the $100 available to her, I suggested that she save $50 and invest $50. It has been more than a year since I gave her this advice, and she has still done nothing. When every step counts, why would she wait? She said that she is not *impressed* by the ability to put $100 away. She thought she should have more than $100 before she started to save and invest.

As a consequence of the dizzying effects of WDS, many of us have procrastinated on numerous wealth-building opportunities, and have therefore missed out on record-breaking wealth opportunities in the stock market. Once we get past that momentary lack of equilibrium (the moments can last minutes, or years), overthinking takes over and makes us think this might be the wrong time to participate in the stock market.

The dizzying effect of WDS makes us out of step. Stereotypically speaking, nobody has ever accused an African-American of being out of step or lacking rhythm. When it comes to managing our money, stereotypically speaking, we are ***arhythmic***. Missing a beat means missing money.

We know how often and how much we get paid. We know when our financial obligations (bills) are due. Too many of my clients have told me that they usually spend more than they make. Yet, they are somehow able to pay bills because the money just appears unexpectedly. Other clients have told me that they cannot stick to a budget because every month there are unexpected bills. As I understand it, *money comes from nowhere and debt comes from nowhere.* Let's be real. People who think money just appears and bills just appear unexpectedly every month, are not in step with their cash flow.

If you are out of step with your cash flow, you cannot determine on your own when and how to be in the stock market. People who have no cash flow rhythm often like to give the impression that they have a sense of how to invest and how risky they can be. Do not worry about impressing your advisor with what you know (or do not know) about money. You will get better advice the more forthright you are. If you have no rhythm, tell them so. They are obligated to advise you based on what you tell them about how you handle money.

Overthinking and procrastination cause you to overthink whether you want to be wealthier. Imagine the absurdity of thinking about and "analyzing" whether you want to be wealthy. You wouldn't do that, would you? Take this test and write down your answer.

Imagine you just won the lottery. You have two choices: Your check will be mailed to you directly overnight or mailed to you in four months. Which would you choose?

Overnight! You probably arrived at that decision within a few seconds. Why? For years you have thought about things you want to do, places you want to go, opportunities you want to pursue, charities you want to support, and gifts you want to give. The decision to take the money now no longer requires thinking or analysis. Let me ask the question again.

If you want wealth, when do you want it?

Overnight or in four months?

If you answered overnight, and you have the ability to but are not currently saving and investing (no matter the amount), you are not being honest with yourself. Four months, four years, or perhaps never are better answers. If you are not on a concrete, deferred gratification plan right now, you do not want wealth right now.

Many of us don't want wealth if we have to change what we are doing with our money. Lotteries are appealing simply because we have a one in 33 millionth chance of winning by doing nothing risky. We can continue living the way we live now, and get rich through luck. In the absence of a lottery prize and in the absence of change, we buy, buy, buy and dream. Buying does not equal wealth, it equals show. Investing equals wealth, but we usually wait months or years after wealth opportunities knock on our doors before we take that step. If we will buy a lottery ticket with no thought and no analysis, why do we overthink investing opportunities? It is a four-letter word in the vocabulary of the fearful African-American female investor. RISK.

14. *Risk Measurement*

Studies done on the investment habits of African-Americans, and the "conventional wisdom" in the investment industry is that *we are adverse to taking risks with our money*. Is this true? Are we really risk-adverse?

I do not think we are risk-averse. I believe we are *risk-measurement challenged* and lacking the right risk measurement tools. When posed with the opportunity to invest, we appear to take hours, days, months, even years before we make the decision to invest. From an advisor's vantage point, it appears as if we are over-analyzing whether we want more money. In actuality, we are overthinking the probability and amount of loss. We are overthinking rather than analyzing because we do not know enough about economics, money management styles, particular money managers, and fund operations to make a decision comfortably. Wealth Disorientation Syndrome is the reason why, in the absence of wealth, we do not push ourselves to know more.

In the absence of knowledge, there are two alternatives: invest relying on the advice of the professional, or invest after you have done the research. Because most of us will not do the research, the road to more money, for most African-

American women, will be through an advisor. (Here's a secret: The road to more money, for *most* people, will be through an advisor).

There is another alternative to doing one's own research, or using an advisor. Unfortunately, it is the alternative most of us choose — do absolutely nothing. Wealth opportunities scare those who suffer from Wealth Disorientation Syndrome. The woman who needs more money but is frightened of investing and thinks the best alternative is for *her* to think about all her options for wealth-building opportunities, is fooling herself.

The stock market existed long before you were born. We have known of its existence for some time. We know that people make money in the market. At the point you knew people made money in it, if you were truly interested in making money, you would have begun your research then. Now, at the moment of decision, you are going to learn all about economics, money management, fund operations, and stock picking? You are undermining your own plan for wealth if you need money now, but you delay getting started until you learn what professionals already know. Understand that there are thousands of people who make a living making others wealthy. All you need to know is that you need someone who can help you become wealthy.

African American women live lives of risks in the U.S. African-Americans only make-up 13 percent of the U.S. population. But when we look at the homeless populations, residents in the criminal justice system, governmental assistance rolls, and recipients of charity over the holidays, we usually make-up a lot more than our proportionate share. The biggest risk we face is that we will not have the money to live independent of governmental assistance at some point in our lives.

The risk that the government will control our financial destinies is the risk that should be avoided at all costs. History and the present show that we do not prosper under governmental control. Becoming financially dependent on governmental assistance at some point in our lives is not just a possibility, but a probability. Yet, we slide down the slippery slope to dependence when we do not take the time to consider how well we handle the other risks in our lives.

There are certain risks that come with being an African-American woman in the U.S.:

◆ There is a risk that you are born to parents too young to rear you properly.

◆ There is the risk that you are born to a single, non-working young woman who cannot financially provide for you without governmental assistance.

◆ There is the risk that your body is not considered a temple, therefore others violate you, and as a consequence, you violate yourself.

◆ There is the risk that your teachers will not invest their time with you because they do not see you succeeding at anything.

- There is the risk that you do not feel loved or nurtured, therefore your first boyfriend becomes the father of your child before you are ready to have children.

- There is the risk that your parents will not have enough money to send you to college, therefore you don't go.

- There is the risk that you will be denied the jobs you want, but offered the ones you don't want; therefore, in order to survive, you take what is offered, and you endure harassment on the job because you are perceived to have a "bad attitude."

- There is the risk that you will grow up in a household where no one educates you about investing.

- There is the risk that you will work most of your adult life never having anyone approach you about investing.

- There is the risk that you will never educate yourself about investing, and, as a consequence, you retire into poverty.

Maybe you had a happy childhood and got everything you wanted from your parents, but now that you have to provide everything you realize money does not grow on trees.

Whatever hardships you may have endured as an African-American woman, understanding those risks should help you understand that what you earn for conquering risks — money — makes it extremely difficult to voluntarily risk your hard earned dollars in the stock market, even it means gaining wealth. Let's consider some alternatives.

Test 1: Begin with the worst case scenario: you become homeless. What are the chances of your becoming a bag lady? It depends on how dependent you are on your job to support your life style. If you are totally dependent, your chances of becoming a bag lady are great. You can minimize the risk of becoming a bag lady by saving money. There is no risk in saving money because you are not subjecting your money to fluctuating market values in a passport savings account.

Test 2: How much money do you live on a year? How long would it take you, given your financial obligations, to save what you make in annual earnings? It is not unusual for someone grossing $45,000 to have only $100 monthly to save. It would take 37.5 years at $100 monthly to save a year's salary. There is a risk in waiting 37.5 years before you have a year's salary saved. A lot can happen in 37.5 years to derail you from consistently saving $100 monthly; therefore, there is a risk that it probably will not happen. The worst part about it is that even if you saved $45,000, it would not be enough to live on for a year. What $45,000 buys today, you will possibly need about $95,000 to buy 37.5 years from now.

If you realize you need money, but you are afraid of losing it, what can you do to become less afraid? The answers lie in your closet.

My clients want strategies for having more money. They know that I cannot advise them properly until they reveal their current financial situation, i.e. their salary, expenses, savings and investments, and debts. Sometimes women cringe in fear of judgment when they reveal there is little to nothing in savings or investments. They often say, "I don't know where the extra money goes" or "I am afraid to risk my money in the stock market." Despite their fears, I suspect that if I were to walk into their closets, I would find evidence of money that was risked and lost voluntarily to the shoe industry. Thousands of dollars voluntarily risked and lost! When clients buy more shoes than they need, yet fear losing money in the stock market, I know they do not understand the real risks of the stock market.

In their closets, in your closet, are valuable lessons to be learned. Let's take a look inside.

Selection Risk

Inside your closet, I can see that you have at least five pairs of shoes, one of which is a pair of boots. When you went shopping for boots three years ago, you narrowed your selection down to two pairs. One pair was made of suede uppers with wooden soles that were glued on. The cost was $75. You could have saved $175, but you bought the leather, Vibram-soled boots because you knew they were sturdy and would last a long time. What risk did you take when you chose the leather over the suede, the Vibram over the wood? **Selection**. When people fear investing, sometimes they fear that they will *select* the wrong investment. Through experience, you know that leather and Vibram holds up much better in the rain than suede and wood. You made the right selection, but only because in the past, you have made bad selections. Bad experiences inform you of what is good. With experience, you can make the right selection in the stock market. Put your boots back in the closet.

Timing Risk

Your sandals are quite nice! I can see you wearing them instead of your athletic shoes any hot day. Sometimes having your toes out can make the difference in your mood, and your look. Oh, and what if you paint your toenails with the latest shade! In anticipation of Summer you purchased your sandals near the end of Spring, but Spring lingers a little too long. It is just too chilly to wear them. What risk have you taken? **Timing.** You have paid for a pair of shoes you can't wear when you want. You have gained nothing but another pair of shoes, but Summer is right around the corner. If you hold on to them long enough, the right time will come to wear them.

Buying stocks at the wrong time (when the price is high) does not mean that there will not be a time when the stock is more valuable to you. People often sell their investments thinking they know when to do it. The key for long term planning, is to buy and hold, through Spring and Winter, ups and downs.

Capital Risk

Your weekly routine is full of exercise. On Mondays you lift weights. Tuesday, aerobics, Wednesdays, tennis, Thursdays, jogging, Friday, walking, and Saturday, aerobics again. You wear the same athletic shoes six days a week, wearing the same pair for lifting weights, tennis, running, walking and aerobics. At this rate, you find that you have to replace your athletic shoes every two months at a cost of $85 to $100 per pair. You are spending $600 a year on athletic shoes. What risk have you taken? The risk that you continue to lose all your money (**capital**) because the shoes do not last. If you bought a pair for each sport (4), and each pair lasted two years, you would have spent on average $200 a year rather than $600. If you must risk your capital, it is better to risk less for the same return. At $200 a year, you are still in great physical condition, and better financial condition. At $600 a year, your physical condition is great, but you have less money for the same physical fitness.

Market Risk

Styles come and go. Heels get higher and lower. Pastels are in, then patent leather black is the thing. Lace ups, slip-ons, you never know what will be the "in" thing! If you are not interested in being with the "in" crowd, and you need a pair of shoes you can wear with everything, you cannot lose with a pair of loafers. Oh, they aren't that exciting, and no one is going to exclaim, "Hey, great loafers!" but you know that no matter the fad, you can wear them with the confidence of knowing they will not be out of style. When you bought the loafers rather than the pastel platforms, you were trying to avoid the risk that the value of your shoes would be virtually unaffected by the current fashion trend.

What if the entire market for shoes drops (imagine that!)? The price of your loafers and every other pair of shoes will also drop. This is called **market or systematic** risk. It is unavoidable in the long run. The best way to anticipate the rise and fall in prices for platforms and loafers is to examine the beta. Ask your investment advisor to explain a stock's beta. This will help you decide between loafers and platforms.

Legislative Risk

Congratulations! You have just been recognized by your employer as "Employee of the Year" and you will be given a plaque at the Awards Banquet. What will you wear? Your dress shoes, naturally. You choose to wear your black pumps with pointed toes and four-inched spike heels. On a daily basis, you are known to wear flats because you do not have to dress up for work and prefer to be comfortable. As a matter of fact, you cannot remember the last time you had to dress up. It's the night of the Awards Banquet. You are sporting your pumps! Secretly, your feet ache from cramped toes to overextended arches. You wobble up to the mike to find that everyone is looking at you because they have never seen you dressed up. They admire your hair, your accessories, make-up and dress, but as they glance down at your shoes, you read on their faces that no woman in their right minds would wear those shoes!

What risk did you take in wearing pointed toe pumps with four-inch spiked heels? That you would be out of style. The laws of fashion changed, and no one informed you in time. While you were busy being comfortable, fashion laws changed, making your dress shoes virtually obsolete as a fash-ion statement. Sometimes people make investment decisions based on current laws such as taxes or trade laws, and fail to follow how the law develops. As a consequence, their money is affected by a change in the law, not a change in the market or in the investment.

Liquidity Risk

You attended the recent neighborhood auction where one of your neighbors auctioned off a pair of pumps once worn by Tina Turner. You were the highest bidder, therefore for the right to own these shoes, you paid $2,500. Later, you lost your job and with nothing in savings, you decided to sell the shoes for at least what you paid. As you go door to door attempting to sell the shoes, you begin to wonder why no one is buying pumps Tina Turner wore. At the next door, you get another rejection, but this time you ask, "Why don't you want to buy a pair of pumps once owned by Tina Turner?" Your neighbor answers, "This is Nashville, town of the Grand Ole Opry. Had you come by here with a pair of shoes worn by Dolly Parton, we might have something to talk about." The inability to sell your investment means you cannot turn something "hard" into "liquid" cash to use as currency for the purchase of something else. When you purchased Tina Turner's shoes, you did so with the risk that you may not be able to liquidate your asset in a timely fashion.

There are a number of other risks involved in investing including inflation, interest rates, reinvestment, credit, liquidity risks. The point is that risk is comprehensible if you apply what you instinctively know about shopping. You cannot avoid risks when you invest, and you cannot avoid poverty unless you invest.

Implications of Risk

Let's return to the 37.5 years example. $100 monthly put into a savings account amounted to $45,000. Now, measure the risk of *investing* $100 monthly for the same amount of time. No one can guarantee what your investment returns will be in the future, but if you invest properly over many years, you will maximize your money by having it in the stock market. For example, suppose you had invested in a growth fund with moderate or conservative growth. Over the past 37.5 years, the average annual return was 10 percent, some years higher and some years lower. In 37.5 years, you would have over $396,000. The difference between *saving* and *investing* is $351,000. If you could choose between having $45,000 and $396,000, which would you choose? I bet you didn't overthink your response!

If you are adverse to taking risks with your money, it is only because you do not understand that the **biggest risk of all is not being in the market for any significant amount of time**. When you weigh being out of the market versus being in the market, then the obvious choice for wealth-building is to be in the market.

Now, determine the amount of money you need to accomplish your goals. Suppose you want to accumulate $10,000 over the next five years to put a down payment on a house or condo. If you are putting your money in a savings account, you must save on average $166.67 monthly. Again, there is no risk in this account. If you need $10,000, but you do not have $166.67 monthly to save, you must invest to reach your goal. Let's say you only have $90 monthly. If you save $90, you will only have $5,400 for the down payment.

There is a risk you will not get the house because your budget does not allow you to save, therefore you must be more aggressive. How aggressive? A moderately conservative investor might make $90 monthly into $10,000 over five years, but only if she changes her risk tolerance from being moderately conservative to aggressive. The more money you need, and the less money you have to commit to your needs, plus the short time in which to accumulate the money means you need to be more aggressive. Your advisor will help you measure the risk level appropriate for your needs.

As you attempt to measure the level of risk you are willing to take to arrive at your goals, you will know you are overthinking, not analyzing, when you begin feeding yourself WDS excuses such as "*I will wait until I make more money, then I'll invest.*" WDS! WDS! Do not procrastinate on wealth-building opportunities because they are always available, but you may not always be able to participate. Or perhaps you tell yourself: "I won't invest anything until I've purchased the things I want and until I have what I want." WDS! WDS!

If you use your money more for buying rather than investing, you have taken on a number of risks in order to exercise your purchasing power. The one compensation for the risks we take, is to spend our salaries for show — to show we survived the risk of being an African-American woman.

Many of us foster the notion that if we generate a good salary and have an impressive title, we do not have to measure the risks. In fact, African-American women with good salaries and prestigious positions have additional risks — the illusion that current income and prestige guarantee income and real authority. If you are still living outside the wealth-building world, you are getting paid a lot to be in a position without real authority. Start building your own authority through wealth, now.

Making more money through work should not make you feel more secure. Having more money, through investing, should. I have clients who make $100,000 salaries and live paycheck to paycheck. I also have clients who make $35,000 and have several thousand dollars invested in their accounts. When you measure the amount of risk you are willing to take, take into account the fact that many people become wealthy in the stock market knowing a lot less than you say you need to know. Let your advisor help you measure the risk, and help you invest. The risk of not doing so is the risk of becoming a bag lady.

Pitting the two against each other, would you rather be on the road to becoming a bag lady, or be on the road to having a financial advisor to help you invest appropriately? If you chose investing, you have properly measured the risk! Congratulate yourself. You are no longer a stereotypical African-American (preservation) woman (preservation). You are growth-oriented, and on your way to having more money. All you need to do now is give some to get some.

15. *Psyche! You Can't Fool Yourself All the Time.*

Everyday you do not invest you grow poorer, until one day, you will have no money and no way to get more. Chances are, you do not feel that you are poorer today than you were yesterday, but if you haven't invested you are.

Do you remember when a great pair of leather shoes cost $50 (or less)? Now the same quality of shoe costs $100 to $200 per pair. Or maybe you noticed that $50 does not buy what it used to buy. The concept is the same. If you are still trying to buy a great pair of leather shoes for $50, think of the quality of a pair of shoes costing $50 ten years from now. One day, you may not be able to buy a pair of shoes for $50. If you are not investing with the objective of keeping pace with inflation (the reason why prices increase slowly over time), you will feel and probably be more broke than you are today.

When you realize you have no money but the money you earn with each paycheck, and still refuse to change your attitude and behavior about money, you should think of alternative solutions. You hope, pray, chant, and wish. You rely on "guaranteed" cost of living increases from your employer, even though there is no guarantee you'll have a job. You position yourself for another raise or promotion to increase your cash flow, and therefore your ability to buy. You hope that the Social Security Administration will continue supporting retirees (though what you'll actually receive will not be enough to live on). If all else fails, there is welfare, your family, and you can sell your belongings if things get really bad.

Social psychologists have noticed an increase in the interest in astrology during times of financial disappointment. Masters Psychics advertises in magazines for African-American women. Their advertisement states that one of their psychics brought "tremendous" financial success to callers of their 1-900 number at $3.99 per minute. These advertisements and infomercials, with the representation of Dionne Warwick, LaToya Jackson and other sisters have created an overrepresentation of African-American women in astrology marketing. Astrology furthers the 40 acres mentality.

PSYCHE!

Are you trying to fool yourself? Now you know you can't fool yourself for long, and why would you want to do this to yourself anyway? Wake up and look at the sisters on the street begging for help. These women had families. They had clothing, food, shelter, and jobs. At one point they held the same beliefs you hold today. They did not become poor in one day or overnight just because they lost their jobs, their families, or their minds. They are poor because while they worked, they didn't invest or save enough for it to matter. The longer you wait to enact your financial plan, then the more you continue to psyche yourself into feeling like you have it all. There are enough people trying to fool you into this and that. Stop fooling yourself and psyching yourself out. It is time to become your own best friend.

16. *Buying-In Doesn't Necessarily Mean Selling-Out*

We live in a country with a racist, sexist, ageist, heterosexist, you-name-it history. I have heard a number of politically progressive activist-minded sisters tell me that they cannot participate in the capitalist system of corporate ownership through the purchase of stocks because there is a direct correlation between corporate ownership and the exploitation of workers.

For the smart sister who thinks too much but does little around her money matters, think little, and do a lot on this thought: **the most socially responsible thing you can do is invest in yourself.** Let me use Kwame Ture again to illustrate this point. Ture has not lived in the U.S. for many years. He has never had any money. It is easy to live abroad, criticize an economic system, and suggest that the only viable alternative is to radically transform society. We are not going to transform the economic system because we get too much from it. Even if we tried to transform society, we will not do so in time for you have the money you need. Investing for yourself is the most socially responsible thing you can do. If you do not believe that the best thing we can do for our society is take care of ourselves and our families, then we need to have a national discussion on the fundamentals of family, not the evils of capitalism. An overwhelming majority of us know we have to take care of ourselves and our families, that is why we need to participate in the institutions that will allow us the best opportunity to do so. We need to do this whether it is politically acceptable to African-American radicals or not.

If you have determined the amount of money you will invest and want to make a contribution to transforming society (yes, you can do both), you must be critically aware of a message being bantered about by some African-American investment advocates: **Invest where you shop**.

At a recent networking seminar I attended, the speaker asked the audience to raise their hands if they had a Coach bag. Then she asked people to keep their arms up if they were also investing in Coach. Only one hand remained. The message was, invest where you shop.

This might be a good thing, or it might be the most destructive thing we can do if we simply invest where we shop. Apparently, we shop at Nike — 80 million pairs were sold in the U.S. in 1997. Nike is under fire for paying its Indonesian workers 65 to 75 cents per hour to manufacture their shoes costing up to $140. If we simply invest where we shop, we will benefit from "slave labor." If we are going to be African-Americans who are truly seeking transformative change through socially responsible investing, we cannot, as descendants of slaves, receive profits from slave labor. There are a number of places you can go for advice and assistance on socially responsible investing. The first place would be your investment professional.

As long as you choose to live in the United States, and as long as you need money to live the way you want to live, you must invest. As long as you appreciate that people have lived and died for you to be able to participate in all institutions, including the stock market, you must invest. As long as you realize that taking care of yourself is the most socially responsible thing you can do, you must invest. When your investment agenda extends beyond yourself and into social change, you must ask if investing where you shop will actually accomplish that goal. If you have nationality ambivalence that borders on hatred of the U.S. and all its institutions, and cannot bring yourself to invest in the stock market, you could help transform the institutions for those who will invest.

The theme of the October, 1998 issue of *Essence* was Building Black Wealth. As usual in the magazine publication business, there were many advertisements. I classified them into five categories: Cosmetics, Financial Services, Clothes and Accessories, Health and Other (cars, food, etc.) I counted 35 cosmetic ads, 28 in the Other category, 8 in Health, 10 in Clothes and Accessories and in Financial Services, 2! Clearly, financial services institutions are not investing their advertising dollars where they could make the greatest impact with sisters. Many of them are ignoring this simple fact: sisters comprise the fastest growing "minority" population of investors in the country.

According to *Guide to Who's Who and What's What on Wall Street* written by the editors of *The Wall Street Journal*, Morgan Stanley Dean Witter is one of only three major full service brokerage firms in the U.S. Each firm has a dearth of African-American brokers, but Dean Witter deserves some attention from African-American activists interested in transformative change. Why Dean Witter? They once had offices in Sears stores, a positive indication that they were willing to meet "everyday people" where they are. Dean Witter's goal is to have more brokers than any other company. If they succeed, they may be in the position to serve more African-Americans. With this in mind, I requested information from Dean Witter directly, asking the following questions:

1. Has Dean Witter advertised in *Essence* Magazine. If so, how many times, when, and what did the advertisements say?

2. How many Dean Witter brokers are African-American women? How many are African-American men?

3. Is Dean Witter a member of Business for Social Responsibility?

4. Does Dean Witter encourage an ethic of serving economically disenfranchised communities and if so, what is the program, who implements it, and how are these communities attracted to Dean Witter's services?

5. If someone is going to invest, what is the minimum investment amount?

The answers? "No comment." I think that response speaks for itself. If your objective is to begin transformative change one company at a time, decide whether you want to begin with a company that says, "no comment," or one that has made an attempt to reach out to you through advertisements and education.

Essence magazine should be full of advertisements from financial institutions. Four food advertisements surround one recipe section. Clearly, the advertisers recognize we buy food. Thirty-five cosmetics advertisements appear because companies know the U. S. cosmetics industry rakes in $8 billion dollars annually, and that sisters spend three times the amount White women spend on cosmetics (an estimated $75 million is spent on "ethnic" skin care products alone). If we invest more than we spend, will *Essence* become the magazine of choice for financial services companies?

Some people have dogmatically said, "If you are not part of the solution, you are part of the problem." The problem is the lack of financial resources. If you want to be part of the solution, consider becoming an agitator. The Reverend Jesse Jackson needs your help with his Wall Street Project (www.rainbowpush.org). If we agitate from the outside, get employees to agitate from the inside, and a board member to persuade the board to conduct business with a new ethic, can we change these companies? If your answer is "no," you have forgotten that African-Americans have changed every institution we have wanted to change. We can make national the issue of financial independence for African-American women. In so doing, we need to support our own as well as change majority-owned institutions.

Buying Black

Historically, socially-responsible investing has meant "buying Black." When you consciously spend your money in African-American owned businesses, you support the efforts of those who you know have been discriminated against for the same reasons you have been discriminated against: the color of our skin.

There was a time when we wanted African-Americans to succeed just because they were of African descent. You may remember watching a television game show where there was one African-American contestant. You rooted for them just because you knew we rarely appeared on game shows, and therefore rarely, if ever, had the chance to win.

Times have changed. We are not supporting African-American owned businesses like we used to. In order to go down in history as the Legacy Class, we must see to it that our businesses survive within the African-American community and are ready for competition in the larger marketplace. Our efforts pull dollars back into our community.

In a nation of beer guzzlers and countless beer makers, I want to stir your entrepreneurial spirit to reveal how an African-American businessman with an obvious race privilege mentality, competes in the game of business as the only African-Amercan contender. Michael LeBlanc is Chief Financial Officer of Brothers Brewing Company (BBC) in Oakland, California. BBC is a new, African-American-owned microbrewery. LeBlanc believes that people entering business with less resources than others must enter the marketplace ready to conduct a war strategically, aware of your strengths and ready to conquer any threat to your business. Identify your needs and pursue them vigorously, making sure you acquire knowledge, skills, contacts and resources along the way, and clearing the path for those who will come after you. BBC can be reached by calling (510) 208-9400, or visit their website at www.3bbc.com.

If BBC is the lone African-American contestant in the game of beer brewing, and you will root for them as you rooted for the contestant on the game show, then you must shop consciously. There are African-American businesses in every community, and well-meaning brothers and sisters who want to buy Black often don't because they do not know where to begin. C. Diane Howell and Carol Tillman, founders of Black Business Listings and The Nubian Network respectively made businesses out of helping patrons find African-American owned businesses. Black Expos are held throughout the country. Black Chambers of Commerce help support businesses and potential customers. If you are an entrepreneur, and you are concerned about the success of Black-owned businesses, you can create linkages between patrons and businesses owners. Remember, the bottom line is this: **Investing in ourselves is the most socially responsible thing we can do.**

17. *The Church and Your Money*

I met with a woman, 30 years old, divorced with two sons, one age 13, the other age 8. Her expenses were low, and she made about $28,000. She had just over $800 in her former employer's 401(k) plan. After she listed her expenses (which did not include saving or investing money), she had no money left. Her goals were to protect her sons in the event she predeceased them, and contribute to an individual retirement account (IRA). Her budget sheet was blank in all the areas for listing savings. However, in one of the spaces she wrote,"Tithe, $100." If she did not tithe, she would have been able to buy life insurance to protect her sons, and contribute to her IRA. She decided to continue tithing.

A number of my African-American female clients give more money to their churches than they do to themselves and their dependents. When asked why, they respond that it is their religious belief that they should do so. Should sisters tithe if they cannot plan for their retirement or their children's welfare?

If you are tithing *aspiritually* (giving without regard to the damage you are doing to yourself and your children), I encourage you to discuss your financial plans with your minister. Ask him or her to preach on the necessity of tithing in the context of comprehensive financial planning. If a minister preaches giving money to the church, and does not preach caring for one's economic needs, he or she is not serving his or her flock fully. In fact, your church probably receives less than it could because many church members are not planning their finances, and therefore not maximizing their tithing. In other words, the church's building fund can grow only if individual members are building and investing appropriately in themselves.

Whatever it takes to get to heaven, there are things that must be accomplished on earth (can I get an Amen to that?). We need to support ourselves and our institutions simultaneously. Some churches have successful for-profit enterprises, calling into question the necessity for tithing 10%. Here is an idea you can bring to your church if it is reliant on tithing: develop a planned gift campaign.

Churches usually receive the greater percentage of their tithes during the Christmas season, yet fixed expenses are the same throughout the year. A planned gift is paid over a period of years or sometime in the future. One of the reasons why planned gifts are not very popular is because the gift does not address immediate needs. Nevertheless, if the church has a vision for the future, and the church requests tithing for future needs, insist that it meets future needs with present planning and future gifts. There are many ways to make a planned gift.   Let's focus first on the simplest, most recognizable vehicle in our community — life insurance.

Life insurance, especially whole life or fixed universal insurance, has taken some heat lately. Some African-American investment professionals think that African-Americans do not invest because they are relying on the slow growing insurance policies they bought years ago to provide for their loved ones upon death, and a cash value to borrow against while alive. In the Ariel/Schwab study, 37% of the African-American respondents said that they intend to use the cash value in their policies as part of their retirement income. Fifty-eight percent said that they do not intend to use whole or fixed universal life insurance to supplement their retirement. This should be encouraging news, but again, life insurance has come under attack. The problem is not having a policy, the problem is under-utilizing it.

In setting up a planned gift campaign for your church, life insurance can be a great option for the financial stability of the church and the insured. The annual premium can be made affordable. As it stands now, a charitable income tax deduction is allowed for the gift of an existing whole life insurance policy that is equal to the cash surrender value at the time of the gift.

Another possible campaign for planned gifts is for the church to be named as a beneficiary of a retirement account. If a churchgoer has a retirement account and has not chosen who or what will be the beneficiary of the account, the church may be a deserving contender. If the account owner dies and the money is left for his or her estate, a huge tax burden may be imposed. It happens too often that those of us who accumulate money over time, give it to the government upon our deaths because we do not plan for the other possibilities. Rather than let the money go to the government, the account owner could name the church as the beneficiary, then the assets are exempted from the state tax and the church does not pay the income tax when it receives the assets.

When you take these ideas to the church, encourage your minister to talk about the advantages to all of financial planning. Everyone wins in time. Those who like to tithe weekly or monthly can continue to do so. Those who only have $50 to tithe might do better by the church to have a life insurance policy, naming the church as the beneficiary. Those with retirement assets and no spouse or children to leave the money to may do great wonders by naming the church as the beneficiary. You and your estate avoid some, if not all the tax burdens, receive the tax benefits, and utilize the financial vehicles already present in our community.

By breaking the Code of Silence in your church, wonderful things can begin to happen. Imagine that your church institutes a service to help you manage your money. (Allen Temple Baptist Church in Oakland, California, has a federal credit union which serves members of the Oakland Chapter of the NAACP and affiliated churches. It provides real estate and consumer loans, and other services). Aspiritual tithing may cause people to give money to the church knowing that if they lost their jobs the next day, they would be unable to help themselves, let alone the church. Planned giving may be the way to fulfill everyone's desires, spiritually and economically.

18. *A Note to Our College-Bound Youth: The Dreams of a Generation, The Failures of Its Progeny*

Congratulations! You made it through high school demonstrating the ability to earn a college degree. We are proud of you. We want you to succeed, and we want you to make great contributions to your community. If you don't go to college, pursuing a career, generally speaking, will be more difficult. You may be stuck in a dead-end job. You may not make enough money to live the way you want to live. Frankly speaking, you may not be able to afford the lifestyle your parents have accustomed you to. You will probably be worse off because you are not college-educated. This may be difficult for you to understand now because you have not lived on your own as a high school graduate competing for jobs with college-educated people. Before you make the decision not to go to college, think long and hard about who and what got you to where you are right now — your parents, with a lot of love, and a lot of money.

Do you love your parent(s)? Do you appreciate that they have gotten you to where you are today because they care? If so, if they tell you they cannot pay for you to go to the school of your choice, or cannot pay for your tuition anywhere, go to school anyway! Educational loans, unlike credit cards and personal loans, are necessary in the absence of your parents' cash. I have heard many young people say that they didn't go to college, or didn't finish college because their parents could not afford it. If you care about your parents, why would you try to financially drain them for your own quality of life? It would be foolish to bring them down financially, only for the money to run out, and you drop out. Low interest borrowing money for school will be the best borrowing decision you will ever make, not only for your parents and for you, but for the rest of us.

I am in my 30's. I have two college degrees. Some of my older relatives earned bachelor degrees and a few earned advanced degrees. My parents weren't college educated, but their dreams for me were to get a college degree. Why? Not to become an "educated fool," or a member of the "intelligent impoverished," but to have the ability to earn more and increase the wealth. Let's be honest, our parents could have done a lot more for themselves with their money if they had not nurtured us. Collectively, African-American parents have paid for the college education of hundreds of thousands of children at the expense of a comfortable retirement for themselves. As a consequence, many of our parents return to us in their old age because they used their money to support us.

We were their investment. Unfortunately, most of us cannot financially support our parents because we did not build the wealth necessary to do so.

Examine your financial relationship with your parents, and what their future financial contributions will be to you. Your parents want to be in the position to pay for your college education. If they say they cannot, believe them. Begin researching scholarship, grant, loan, and work opportunities, and pay your way through school. Beware of the credit card companies that seduce you into applying for credit cards while you are in school. Their representatives will tell you how much money you are going to make in four years, and that therefore you can afford to pay the interest they will charge you today. Don't take it! It's plastic crack, and crack does not mix with higher education. Last year, an estimated 250,000 people under the age of 25 years old filed bankruptcy. In college, there is a great tendency to do what the in-crowd is doing. The in-crowd is living on credit cards. We beg you to earn your degree, and enter the workforce with as little consumer debt as possible. If you minimize your consumer debt, you will be able to maximize your wealth.

We, the African-American community, have decided what our financial agenda is for you and the next generation.

- ♦ We want you to be college educated, if you possess the discipline and intellect.

- ♦ We want you to have greater earning potential.

- ♦ We do not want you to be broke; therefore we

are going to teach you about money.

♦ We do not want you to become the "intelligent impoverished."

♦ We want you to become part of the Legacy Class.

You and your classmates will be the ones to see to it that our community is better off than it is today. Let's agree that the one thing we want to pass on to you and your children is the value of education, and the ability to build wealth. The future looks bright with you educated and wealthy.

For more information about funding college costs, contact the U.S. Department of Education, Student Financial Assistance Programs at (800) 4-FED-AID and request their current pamphlet "Funding Your Education." **Remember, invest in yourself because there will never be a better investment than the one you make in yourself.**

19. *Written Exclusively for the Busy Sister*

GET A FINANCIAL ADVISOR! SHE'LL DO THE WORK FOR YOU!

There is a debate brewing in the financial services community about how financial advisors, counselors, and planners should be paid — fee or commission or both. Generally speaking, if you are just getting started with your plan, and you are committing a small amount of money to your plan, paying commission will cost you less. If strategizing your plan is a complicated task because you have many things in place already and you are going to commit large sums of money to your plan, a fee may cost you less than a commission.

When you are interviewing advisors, ask them how they are paid, and tell them about your current situation. Ask them for the pros and cons to you, the client, of paying commission or fees. You should work with a planner who exhibits no conflict of interest between your needs and theirs. It is impossible to avoid potential conflicts of interest. If the advisor charges a commission, ask what it is, whether they are paid more if you choose riskier investments, and if they participate in sales contests. If the advisor charges a fee, ask for an estimate of how long it will take to complete your plan. Multiply the hours by the fee (unless it's a flat fee) and if the costs outweigh the financial benefit to you, choose commission. Sometimes, people settle for a fraction of a plan because they can't afford the fee for an entire plan. You don't have to settle for a fraction. Commission is an alternative.

20. *A Note to My Brothers — If It Takes a Village...*

This book was written especially for smart sisters who think to much and do too little. I have told some of my African-American male clients about this book, and they have responded, "Make sure you include something for the brothers." I would have written this entire book for brothers and sisters if I could have. Unfortunately, my experience in advising brothers is minimal. I have telephonically introduced my services to many brothers who commit to an initial meeting, and most do not show for their appointments. If they meet with me, many do not take my advice. If I have detected a pattern of behavior among brothers that is predictable and profound, it is that they do not talk to me or other investment professionals. Period. To my disappointment, I confirmed my conclusion with a brother and former financial services professional. He told me that the brothers who actually spoke with him, did not do business with him. As a consequence, he refused to meet with brothers.

You may know the African proverb, "It takes a village to raise a child." In this context you are part of the village responsible for ensuring the success of the next generation. Sisters are seen as leeches on the American economy, and brothers are seen as forsaking their offspring. If it takes a village to raise a child, it takes a village to create the Legacy Class. We must begin talking with each other about money.

In my experience advising men, I have concluded that men do not know more about money matters than women. However, brothers have confessed that they should know more about money than they do, because they are men. Some of my clients have told me that brothers may not want to share with a woman the fact that they have no money. Maybe we are all just keepers of the Code of Silence.

Whatever it is that is keeping you silent, try to work through it if you want more money. A good advisor who works with African-Americans probably knows how you are feeling. They will not be surprised to discover you do not have as much as you would like to have. They will not be judgmental, because everyone who works with an advisor has some problem, question or issue. Maybe that is the issue, determining whether your lack of knowledge about money matters is a "problem." If you do not know enough about money to know whether you are on the right track, and you are doing nothing about it, you have WDS. Your advisor can re-direct you toward wealth.

IV. *What's a Smart Sister To Do?*

Remember our history. Our ancestors were brought here to enrich others. When that plan ended, we were here to comprise the lower economic class. As a result, we have less money than we should. Dr. King's Poor People's March 30 years ago did not result in guaranteed income for the present poor. Too many of us who are not poor today, will be members of the *future poor* unless we break the **Code of Silence** about the cultural, political, religious and social influences causing some of us to have *Wealth Disorientation Syndrome.*

Think about the present. The nation harbors hostility toward us as the economy soars. In the news, we are often used as examples of leeches, using and abusing the welfare system in lieu of saving and investing. Rarely do we read or hear about trends that demonstrate we comprise the fastest growing group of "minority" investors, or we are contributing more money and time to our communities. To be a part of a nation that is number one in wealth and number one in poverty tells us we can be wealthy or poor. The major African-

American civil rights and radical change movements agree that poverty (not wealth) is our major problem. We have not known how to talk about saving, investing, and insuring because we have not fully utilized the financial services industry. Rest assured, this will change.

The past and the present are not that different. One hundred and thirty-four years ago, we wanted 40 acres and a mule. Today, we say we want the same thing. While addressing the 1998 NAACP convention, Vice President Al Gore proclaimed that economic empowerment is the last civil rights frontier. One hundred and thirty-four years ago, it was the first civil rights frontier. Past, present, first, last, up, down, back and forth. It's dizzying, and it keeps us thinking too much and doing too little.

We have lived with the Code of Silence, and it has left us mute. The Code served its purpose when our community had no money. We confused our muteness with being deaf. We heard, but claim we didn't hear. We heard, but we dismissed it because we didn't have money. Today, we generate money! We are generating hundreds of billions of dollars, and marching to the house of the future poor at the same time. As we have lived with the Code, plastic crack has been introduced into our homes and colleges. We have admitted that most of us who make money are fair or poor savers. Many of us ignore the messages directed toward African-American women because silence itself can be deafening. When the moment of personal economic decision comes, we feel nervous, tense, anxious, dizzy, sick, disoriented. We procrastinate. We get closer to the poor house, but we don't know just how much closer we have gotten.

What's a smart sister to do to avoid becoming a member of the future poor?

You are going to create your own *econo-culture*. An econo-culture is bringing the economy into your consciousness; tuning out negative messages about sisters being leeches and tuning in to messages, resources, and professionals already in existence.

I know a sister who had been fired from her job. When she was fired, she had no savings, no retirement, no mid-term investments, no insurance for her loved ones, and credit card debt. She created an econo-culture, and a year later she has a money market account, an individual retirement account, money in a 401(k), and no credit card debt. She also bought life insurance to protect her loved ones.

That sister is yours truly. I created an econo-culture that was difficult to understand, at first. The ability to step out of one's areas of familiarity is initially difficult. Your econo-culture may prove challenging, too. Trust me when I say, that it will not be as challenging as living without income. If you suffer from Wealth Disorientation Syndrome, I will provide you with the strategy that will redirect you toward wealth. It begins with the creation of your own econo-culture.

12 Steps in Creating a Personal Econo-Culture

1) **Get a professional financial advisor.** Your advisor will help lead you through the forest of financial information and vehicles, and coach you as you play Financial Hopscotch. I am aware that many of us do not trust others with advice about our money. If you trust the opinions of your friends and colleagues, ask them for a referral. If they are not working with anyone, contact the Coalition of Black Investors (COBI) at www.cobinvest.com and request an African-American professional in your area.
   You can also use the telephone book and call people. Ask them how they get paid, if they require you to have a certain amount of money and whether they have read this book. My concern is that you might reach someone who has no experience working with African-American women. You can help them understand by recommending this book, and then they will be more prepared the next time a sister calls.

2) **Subscribe to *Black Enterprise*.** Many clients have told me that financial planning is for "white folks" and everyone they see talking about money is white. *Black Enterprise* is full of "black folks" writing about money: how to make it through enterprise, and how to make it through investing. For more in-depth information from black folks, read *Money Talks: Black Finance Experts Talk to You About Money* by Juliette Fairley. If you cannot afford to subscribe to or buy any publication listed, make time to

go to the library.

3) **Subscribe to *Fortune, Money Magazine, Smart Money, or Worth***. Read an issue of the *Wall Street Journal* on occasion. These publications are full of "white folks" but so is everything else we consume. Do not let representations of white people be the reason you do not consume valuable information. There is a "wealth" of information in these magazines because this is where most financial companies advertise.

4) **Stop shopping with impulse spenders**. Spending time where you do not need to be, and spending time with impulsive people in places of economic destruction is a waste of time and money.

5) **Listen to *Market Place* on Public Radio International and National Public Radio**. They discuss the state of the economy and issues that affect you, in ways you can and will understand.

6) **Join *Money* Book Club**. It is great to have a catalogue come to your door with opportunities for ordering new information relevant to whatever your money information needs are. The Money Book Club can be reached by writing them at Money Book Club, Camp Hill, Pennsylvania 17012-0001 or www.moneybookclub.com.

7) **Contact the National Association of Investment Clubs** for clubs in your area, and determine whether the clubs provide the type of education you need to understand stock picking.

8) **Stop being a Money Lender**. Encourage those who con-

sistently borrow money from you to stop begging. Give them the telephone number of your financial advisor.

9) **Watch TV**. There are numerous television shows on money, such as the *Nightly Business Report* on PBS. Find one that you think is entertaining and informative and watch it often.

10) **Buy a copy of Barron's** *Dictionary of Finance and Investment Terms*. Refer to it to help you through the "foreign" language of money.

11) **Turn to the back of this book.** There is a sample letter you can send to a financial institution which should provoke them to respond favorably to African-American women. Please send me a copy, along with your feedback of "*Beyond 40 Acres and Another Pair of Shoes.*" I have received a number of requests to write on a number of financially-related topics. Let me know what you need to know to improve your financial life.

12) **Create your budget and financial plan today, not tomorrow.** Buy a book that helps you develop your plan, talk to others, find a professional advisor. Take the time you spend considering whether to go to the next shoe sale and start investing in yourself. Every moment you delay is one less dollar you'll earn towards your future.

When you begin to bring knowledgeable people and their resources into your world, what they say competes with your inner voice of skepticism, and with conflicting messages you have heard from others. All this talk can exacerbate WDS.

Eliminate from your present culture impulsive spenders, consistent borrowers, unnecessary shopping, and ignore the negative messages you feed yourself. Remember, you have dreams, and a vision. You can live those dreams, if you prepare properly.

Keep *Beyond 40 Acres and Another Pair of* Shoes by your bills and refer to it monthly as you pay others. If you create an econo-culture, and have not increased your net worth a year from now, write and tell me why it did not happen. It worked for me, and that is why it will probably work for you. There are never any guarantees when it comes to how much money you will have. The one thing that is sure is that you have the control.

Thank you for your participation in the movement to address the financial concerns of women of African descent. We have fought for many rights, and won. We have victoriously challenged many oppressive systems, and brought them down. We can easily handle personal finance. If each of us teaches one of us, and we are apprised of the national "score" on the financial independence of African-American women, financial victory is ours.

We know how to lead, we know how to organize. We know how to bring a project to a close having met our goals. With money — imagine the possibilities. We know the obstacle is the reliance on broken promises. We know the salvation has been in material things. Our culture lived in silence about money, but now, we speak and hear. We know what we must move beyond, and we know what we need and why. I believe that one day, you will live the rest of your life without financial worry. Why?

You are the **Legacy Class**. You have the success of many women behind you, and the advice and assistance of those before you. You are creating your own econo-culture, bringing the good in, and dispensing with the bad. I cannot wait until the day when we begin rebuilding and restoring public schools to their original glory. I cannot wait until we can better support candidates for political office. I cannot wait until we level the playing field of competition in business and in education, where we do not have to worry whether we can succeed. I cannot wait until we have enough resources to affect domestic and foreign policy so that no more Black people are starving. I know I am not alone. We cannot wait to make our dreams a reality, and you can no longer wait to put your financial plans into effect. We are ready to move *Beyond 40 Acres and Another Pair of Shoes*.

100 Years from Today

I shudder to think that just 100 years ago, as a Yoruba-American, I would have probably grown up in a community where there were no safe schools to attend, no safe parks to play in, no opportunity to go to college, and even if I had worked a decent job all my life, no retirement savings. Had it not been for the Legacy Class, every civil rights organization would still have economic empowerment on their agendas.

We owe gratitude to those smart sisters who decided to create a legacy for their offspring. Through their efforts to change their existence, they changed our culture. As a matter of fact, I would not have been able to start this magazine without my inheritance. In my grandmother's diary, she said that she was inspired to build a "little estate, not huge, but enough to give Marcia something to start a business, if she wants..." Thank you, Nana.

A funny thing happened the other day when I took my daughter to school. There was a line of White parents with their children, trying to get their children into the public schools. It is remarkable to find that all types of people are returning to metropolitan areas to educate their children in what 100 years ago used to be called "inner city" schools.

"Inner city" was code for inferior. Through effort, we made them superior, and now, everyone wants in.

Every morning I work, I habitually get a cup of coffee from the cafe downstairs. This morning a group of five women who appeared to be in their fifties, were sitting down, drinking coffee, and playing cards. They were laughing uproariously, and they were all dressed casually, which meant to me they were not thinking about going to work. Everyone who knows me knows I am nosy, so being my nosy self, I approached them, introduced myself and what I do, and asked them if they were going to get fired for not being at work. They looked at me and laughed even louder than before. One of them said, "We haven't worked the past three years!"

I ran back to my office to meet with my intern from the Barbara Jordan School of Political Science at the University of Texas. She informed me that U.S. Senate hopeful Karen Peters, the 50th woman of African descent to launch a viable U.S. Senate campaign, shocked the state, and the nation, when she announced that she would be the first to fund the entire campaign with her own money! Just as her announcement hit the papers, her opponents dropped out of the race.

Life is good at home, but no time can change Mother Nature. Another drought hit the Sudan, leaving hundreds of thousands of people thirsty and hungry. The NAACP-Worldwide, shipped in its own jets, cargos of food and drink to help the Sudanese during this period of crisis.

As you are reading my column, I know it is hard for you to believe that there was a time when we had no collective plans for our money. My grandmother used to tell me that her contemporaries found it hard to believe that slavery existed. She always told me that you cannot go anywhere if you do not know where you have been. It's good to see that we know where we have been, because it looks like we just arrived!

Marcia Barnnson,
Founder and Editor-in-Chief
Black Gentry Magazine
January, 2098

A Note to the Investment Industry and its Investment Professionals

As an investment professional, I know that many of my colleagues, especially those who are not African-American, do not have many clients who are African-American women. Many of us work in institutions where the only goal is to open a certain number of accounts, and bring in a certain number of dollars. The prevailing notion is that one's job is well done when the accounts are opened and the money is deposited. We operate under the misconceptions that African-American women:

1. Do not have money;
2. Do not invest, even if they have money;
3. Do not invest enough money for you to make a living, if they invest;
4. If they invest enough to make it worth your while, may not invest with you because you are not deemed trustworthy;
5. Even if you are trustworthy, you are not African-American, and African-Americans would rather en-

trust their money to other African-Americans;

6. Perceive your firm as lacking diversity and not politically progressive or socially responsible. Therefore, it is useless to try to attract business from African-American women.

Regardless of your background, regardless of the firm you are with, you might make your services known and available to everyone with money. Why? African-American women cannot wait until the industry changes its way of doing business or wait until the entire industry changes its color. African-American women need financial services now. Lawyers know the importance and the cost of their services; therefore, they have ethical standards to assist those who cannot offer to pay them. Our services are just as important and in some cases as expensive as the services of a lawyer. Economically disenfranchised people need justice in the form of accessible education and assistance in making good financial choices. By and large, the industry has given the impression that African-American women are not worthy of your services. I am encouraged to see that it is changing.

African-Americans, in greater numbers, are using the services of financial professionals of all persuasions. Thanks to *Black Enterprise*, the Coalition of Black Investors, the National Association of Investment Clubs, money managers Cheryl Broussard and Eddie Brown, coach Glinda Bridgeforth, The Ariel Funds founder John Rogers, TV host and author Kelvin Boston, journalist and author Juliette Fairley, financial planner and author Brooke M. Stephens and a host of other individuals and entities. African-Americans are becoming more aware of the fact that we have a choice about where our money goes.

If you want to be an investment professional worthy of our business, I suggest you consider adopting a personal ethic and code of conduct to attract the business of underserved communities.   If you can negotiate the amount of money you are expected to bring in every year, and you want to act with social conscience and caring, reach out to us. Begin by understanding who we are. A key rule of the industry is, "know your customer." You can begin knowing African-American women by understanding our experiences. We come with a history of economic exploitation, deprivation, and false governmental promises. We have become scapegoats for America's economic ills. Many of us see you as being driven by greed, and sometimes we take issue with how you are paid because hardly anyone has reached out to us to educate us on how you do business. If you are aware of these issues and concerns you can become a most trusted advisor.

I understand that it is not easy to change the way you do business, especially if you are associated with a company that does not have the same ethic toward underserved communities. One way you can assist your company in attracting African-American women to your services, is to encourage the decision-makers to become members of Business for Social Responsibility (BSR). BSR is a national association of businesses providing assistance to companies seeking to implement policies and practices that contribute to the "long-term, sustained and responsible" success of their enterprises. Contact BSR for membership information at www.bsr.org.

In addition to adopting a personal code of conduct and encouraging your company to become a member of BSR, encourage your company to advertise regularly in magazines such as *Essence*. Practically every African-American woman has read this magazine at least once. *Essence* is not a fashion magazine; it is a magazine for the betterment of African-American women. *Essence* typically runs advertisements for everything from beauty products to health care products to automobiles. Your company has a great chance of getting noticed with regular, persuasive advertisements featuring African-American women. The October, 1998 issue was about building wealth. There were only two advertisements from financial institutions. What an opportunity missed!

The African-American market has been ignored by most wealth-building companies. For example, during the 4th Annual Soul Train Lady of Soul Awards (which recognizes the top African-American contemporary female recording artists — and you know there are many), a number of companies purchased air time, including Intellicredit and 1-800-BAR-NONE. Both companies assist people with damaged credit to buy cars. There was not one wealth-building commercial. That is a pity. If your company has a national advertising budget, your company could compete for the millions of dollars generated by these recording artists and their producers.

There are more young African-American self-made millionaires than ever, and no substantive brokerage presence. Bill Cosby, in his pursuit of owning a socially responsible professional football team remarked that the locker room was full of "girly" magazines, and not one money magazine. The market, so to speak, is practically untapped. Here is your opportunity to act ethically and increase your bottom line simultaneously. We look forward to seeing you where we are!

Sample Letter to A Financial Institution

Date
Company
ATTN: Director of Marketing
Address

Dear Marketing Director:

    I recently read a book entitled *Beyond 40 Acres and Another Pair of Shoes: For Smart Sisters Who Think Too Much and Do Too Little About Their Money.* I am an African-American woman about to make some major decisions about my money. I regularly read _____ (magazine, newspaper, on-line source) which is written for African-American women. I have noticed advertisements from _____, but I have not seen your company advertise there. I use _____ (magazine, newspaper, on-line source) as a shopping mall for all sorts of things from clothes, to books, cosmetics, careers to personal finance. I am concerned about the lack of information in _____ (magazine, newspaper, on-line source) because it leads me to believe your company is not interested in having me as a customer. Nevertheless, before I jump to conclusions, please send me information about your company, and why I should do business there. I am also requesting similar information from your competitors.

    Thank you, in advance, for the materials. I look forward to receiving the information within two weeks. If I like what I see, I will get in touch with a local representative of your company for additional information. I look forward to having a long-lasting business relationship.

Sincerely,

Name
cc: Pamela Ayo Yetunde

About the Author

Pamela Ayo Yetunde, a financial consultant with a New York investment firm, works with individuals, small business owners, and not-for-profit organizations. She has a B.A. in Journalism from Ball State University and a law degree from Indiana University School of Law-Bloomington. She has worked as a journalist in The Netherlands, a political organizer, and a human rights advocate.

In 1998, she founded **BW2000**, an educational movement for African-American women interested in collective action backed with money. *Beyond 40 Acres and Another Pair of Shoes: For Smart Sisters Who Think Too Much, and Do Too Little Around Their Money Matters* is the natural outgrowth of that movement.

A native of Indianapolis, Indiana, Ms. Yetunde currently resides in Oakland, California and can be reached at pay@smartsisters.com.

For additional copies of this book, please send check or money order for $20 (includes S&H and tax) to:

Marabella Books
4096 Piedmont Avenue PMB 307
Oakland, CA 94611
(510) 337-3262

http://www.smartsisters.com